Dodge City

Dodge City

THE MOST WESTERN TOWN OF ALL

Odie B. Faulk

New York
OXFORD UNIVERSITY PRESS
1977

Copyright © 1977 by Oxford University Press, Inc.

Library of Congress Cataloging in Publication Data
Faulk, Odie B
  Dodge City, the most Western town of all.
  Includes index.
  1. Dodge City, Kan.—History. I. Title.
F689.D64F38   978.1'76   76-51710
ISBN 0-19-502225-4

Printed in the United States of America

FOR CARL N. TYSON
who taught me about Kansas

Preface

As Hitler's troopers stormed into Poland in 1939, advertisements appeared in German newspapers for a new movie from America, "Der Draufganger von Dodge City" (The Daredevil of Dodge City). According to this ad, Dodge was a city of "adventure and women of ill repute; the city of the famous dancer of the Red Lantern cabaret; the meeting place of the sons of Buffalo Bill; and the city of robbers, bandits, and pimps." Today, thanks to other movies and to television shows, the image of Dodge City is still one of unrestrained lawlessness and violence, of gamblers and prostitutes, of gunfights in the streets and "a man for breakfast" every morning.

Dodge City was a wide-open town during its early years. Established in 1872 on the western edge of the military reservation known as Fort Dodge, it served as a depot for the Santa Fe Railroad, then laying tracks along the old Santa Fe Trail. However, few farmers settled nearby, for the climate of southwestern Kansas seemed too dry for raising profitable crops. Had farmers settled there in large numbers, they and their families might have provided stability and staidness. Dodge City therefore was left sitting in a vast plain of grass that was the home of Comanche, Kiowa, and Kiowa-Apache Indians, millions of buffalo, a few soldiers trying to maintain the peace, and buffalo hunters killing millions of bison and needing a place to sell their hides, buy supplies, and vent their enthusiasm for unrestrained fun.

To serve these buffalo hunters, as well as the soldiers at Fort Dodge, merchants moved to the new town, along with gamblers, saloonkeepers, and prostitutes. These residents could not afford a staid, moral community because the hunters would only go where they could indulge their pleasures. The same situation pertained after 1876, when, with buffalo disappearing and the Indians contained on reservations, cowboys began arriving in Dodge with herds of longhorns to be shipped to Eastern packing houses. They also were young men unfettered by civilized restraints, their pockets full of money, and their hearts set on a roaring spree.

Yet from the moment of its founding, Dodge had forces of reform at work: prohibitionists forming temperance societies, moralists working to end the gambling, and church members wanting to close the houses of prostitution. Existing side-by-side with the immoral element were people forming a literary society, a band, churches, volunteer fire companies, and benevolence groups. Schools and churches were built, along with a courthouse and jail. But reform and culture were hampered by the ties between the town and the cattle industry; only when the trail closed and the cowboys stopped coming would Dodge become a copy of other Kansas towns.

In retelling the history of Dodge City, I have attempted to avoid the romantic nonsense so often associated with its peace officers and shady characters, as well as to explain why the people there have commercialized the sordid aspects of their past. In preparing this book I have incurred numerous debts, which I freely acknowledge. I owe a great debt to the administrators and staff of the Kansas State Historical Society; the holdings there are so rich that I believe no book can be written about Kansas without the help of this organization—which they freely and gladly give. Moreover, I was aided by librarians at the University of Kansas Library (Kansas Collection), the Kansas State Library, and the Wichita State University Library. Workers in the Ford County Clerk's office gave valuable assistance, as did the staff of the Dodge City Chamber of Commerce. And, as always, the staff of the Oklahoma State University Library provided valuable assistance.

Individuals who have helped me include Drs. Jimmy M. Skaggs and William Unrau of Wichita State University, and Dr. James M. Smallwood of Oklahoma State University. I have dedicated the book to Carl N. Tyson who long ago explained to me that when God needed a garden He created Kansas. Two final debts I here acknowledge: as always I owe much to the fine editorial staff of Oxford University Press, particularly Mr. Sheldon Meyer; and my wife did her usual excellent job of proofreading and making suggestions for improvement.

Stillwater, Oklahoma   ODIE B. FAULK
December 1, 1976

Contents

Dodge City

A Country of
Fine Appearance

Early in June of 1542, Francisco Vásquez de Coronado led a small party of thirty mounted Spaniards, along with ten footmen and servants, northward across what today is the Panhandle of Oklahoma into southwestern Kansas. Their quest was for a fabled land they called the Gran Quivira. There, according to stories told them by a captive Indian, they would find a river five miles wide containing fish as big as horses; the canoes on the river had sails, and the chief of the land took an afternoon nap under a tree adorned with golden bells that tinkled musically as the breeze blew through them. Even the humblest peasant in the Gran Quivira ate from golden dishes, and enjoyed all manner of precious metals and jewels.

Despite the thoughts of such wealth, these Spaniards took note of the geography they were traversing. Their journey from the Rio Grande Valley of central New Mexico had led them eastward into the Panhandle of Texas onto what they called the *Llano Estacado*—the Staked Plains. This was a high, flat country that began far to the south and stretched northward to Canada, a land "so level and smooth," wrote one of the Spaniards, "that if one looked at them [buffalo] the sky could be seen between their legs, so that if some of them were at a distance they looked like smooth-trunked pines whose tops were joined."

Across this plain the Spaniards trekked until they came to the valley of the Arkansas River. Suddenly they were confronted by a broken country called by modern geographers the Finney and Great Bend Lowlands. To the north and south of these lowlands, the Great Plains stretched from horizon to horizon, but in between were water, trees, and many varieties of wild game. This abrupt change in their surroundings greatly impressed the Spaniards. One of them, Juan Jaramillo, paused to note in his journal that this was "a country of fine appearance the like of which I have never seen anywhere in Spain, in Italy, or in any part of France." Trying to describe it for European readers, he continued, "It is not a hilly country, but has table-lands, plains, and charming rivers with fine waters. It greatly pleased me, and I am of the belief that it will be productive of all sorts of commodities."

What these Spaniards were crossing was the broad swath of land to the east of the Rocky Mountains, a vast plains formed by silt carried out of the mountains. The land slopes gradually downward as it moves eastward from the Rockies, and the annual rainfall increases as the elevation decreases. Despite the relative sameness of the land, the Great Plains is a region alive to the seasons of the year. In the winter, while high in the mountains to the west snow is piling up many feet deep, cold winds blast down from the far north, coating the land with snow that blows and swirls and piles up in drifts. These blizzards (technically, to be so called the temperature has to drop approximately twenty degrees from the previous day's average) are intensely cold and usually last several days. All life comes to a standstill, for to go out in a blizzard is to get lost and freeze. The spring begins with *chinooks*, warm southerly breezes which can melt a foot of snow overnight and which bring water rushing out of the mountains with yet more silt to form another layer on the plains. Then come weather fronts from the Pacific, triggering violent storms, many containing tornadoes, which dump inches of rain and, often, large hail which mauls the land. This moisture brings the grass to life. Usually called "short-grass," this is vegetation that seldom grows higher than twelve to sixteen inches, for the scant rainfall does not provide enough moisture to allow the extensive root systems needed by taller varieties. The more level the land, the more the grass dominates. However, where the land is broken, other kinds of plants grow—gnarled mesquite trees, thorny shrubs, and cactus—while along the banks of occasional rivers and creeks cottonwood trees can be seen in profusion.

Summer on the plains is hot, the wind coming predominantly from the south. A hot, dry breeze blowing up from Mexico can parch everything in its path. Then the grass turns a golden brown, but it is rich and nutritious and supports many kinds of animals. The autumn brings yet another series of rain storms as moisture-laden winds blow up from the Gulf of Mexico to meet cold fronts coming down from the Arctic. When the southerly breezes dominate, the days are warm and lazy, a time of Indian summer when leaves on the trees along river and stream turn gold and red; but when the northerly winds blow, there is a bite to the air that tells animals, birds, and man that winter soon will clap its icy hand on the land. The newcomer to this region soon learns to know the wind, for it determines temperature, gives needed water, or sears all into semidesert.

Crossing the land from mountains in the west to gentler land in the east are several rivers: the Missouri, the Platte, the Arkansas, the Cimarron, the Canadian, the Red, the Trinity, and the Brazos. Of these the Arkansas is midway between the Gulf of Mexico and Canada, a stream born high in the central Rockies and fed year-round by melting snow. Down it rages and tumbles through granite-imprisoning walls, carving Royal Gorge just as it emerges from the mountains to escape and flow across the plains. In the spring it sprawls across several hundred yards of territory as melting snow and rains cause it to leave its banks and spread to the surrounding countryside. For the remainder of the year, however, it is content to flow only a few feet deep, doing its eternal work of transporting silt out of the mountains. Entering Kansas in present-day Hamilton County, it flows eastward through the Finney Lowland, the width of its valley varying from twenty-five to forty miles. Near Dodge City, however, it inexplicably turns to the northeast to form the Great Bend Lowland before curving back to the southeast to depart from the state at Wichita. Prior to the many irrigation projects that presently sap its strength, the Arkansas frequently changed channels as silt piled up at one point or another; thus it is labeled an anastomosing stream.

Because there is water in this river at all times of the year, the Arkansas Valley is frequented by numerous animals and birds. Beneath the ground lives the ground squirrel, a bright-eyed, whistling, buff-colored rodent marked by dark brown stripes; it burrows into the earth to make its home, thereby loosening, aerating, and mixing the soil. More numerous was the black-tailed prairie dog, which lived in "towns" containing thousands of their number; because they piled the earth around the entrance to their burrows, they promoted the growth of plants that otherwise could not penetrate the grassy plains. Some of these prairie dog towns occupied thousands of square miles and housed millions of rodents. Moles and gophers likewise dig into the earth. These small animals are at the bottom of the food chain, subsisting on various types of seeds and insects. Above the ground are millions of other small rodents, the prairie deer mouse, the harvest mouse, and the grasshopper mouse. Enemy to all these rodents is the prairie rattler which, because it cannot regulate its body temperature by sweating, has to burrow underground to escape the heat of the midday.

Still larger is the jack rabbit, one of the pioneer folk heroes of the West. Along the Arkansas River two types of jack rabbits meet and intermingle: the white-tailed jack of the north country, which turns white in winter, and the black-tailed jack of the south, which stays the same color year-round. With large, bulging eyes and big, sensitive ears, the jack rabbit easily detects predators, which it escapes by means of its speed or its coloration that enables it to blend into its surroundings. They, like the burrowing animals, eat grasses and forbs.

Another small animal feeding on vegetation is the skunk, thousands of which can be found on the plains, their striped tails waving. Few meat-eaters attack the skunk because of its system of chemical defense, the great horned owl being the only exception. Each of these animals attempts to find its niche in nature. Each has its food supply and each its method of defense: burrowing, running, camouflage, or chemical. And all need protection, for there are many predators.

The badger, the largest member of the weasel family, noted for the white stripe running from its nose down its back, spends most of its life digging out ground squirrels and other rodents. Rarely does it attack anything else, but when it is attacked it fights back with ferocity. Its kin, the black-footed ferret, prefers prairie dog burrows. Its dark mask covering gleaming eyes, the ferret lives its life cycle in relative ease because of the abundance of its food supply.

Above ground, roaming widely across the plains, is yet another folk hero, the coyote. Often called a scavenger because it feeds on the kill of the wolf and other large hunters, the coyote nonetheless is a skilled hunter capable of killing rodents, rabbits, and other small game. Moreover, it eats almost anything—insects, snakes, and birds. Protected by its size from smaller predators and by its coloration and speed from larger ones, it survives cold winters and hot summers by cunning and craft. Robert M. Wright, who was in the vicinity of Fort Dodge prior to the arrival of many whites, commented later, "There were big gray wolves and coyotes by the thousands, hundreds of the latter frequently being seen in bands, and often from ten to fifty grays in a bunch."

Wolves were the terror of the plains, for thousands of them inhabited the region at mid-nineteenth century. Most of these were dark gray, although a few white ones sometimes drifted down from the north and, occasionally, a wolf of almost blue color might be

seen. Their skins were prized by the Indians. Wolf packs followed
the buffalo, killing the very young, the old, and the sick. Wright
noted that a terror of the plains was rabid wolves, for they frequently became infected.[1] Another canine hunter of the area was
the small kit fox, pale buff in color, which moved rapidly across
the plains in search of rabbits and rodents. And an occasional
grizzly would wander out from the mountains; nothing bothered
it because of its size and its ugly temperament.

Wolves, coyotes, and other large meat-eaters frequently went in
search of two large animals which lived on the grasslands: pronghorn antelope and buffalo. The pronghorn, which is distinct from
the true antelope of Africa, did not rely on concealment or coloration for survival. Rather it sought the open ground as it fed, for it
wanted to see danger afar and outrun it. Weighing about 100
pounds when fully grown, the pronghorn had heavily built legs,
lungs of great capacity, and a large heart; these enabled it to run
as fast as sixty miles an hour for short periods, and thirty miles an
hour for long periods.

The Indians early learned that the pronghorn was a curious animal, one which investigated anything out of the ordinary. Therefore the Indian hunter would lie in the grass and raise a stick with
feathers attached to it. When the animal approached to satisfy its
curiosity, it could be shot with bow and arrow. The young of the
pronghorn weighed about five pounds at birth. Instinct compelled
them to lie very still in the grass until the mother came to feed it.
Within a week of its birth, however, the young calf could run
with its mother and was capable of outrunning a man.

The buffalo, or American bison, relied on its size and weight for
protection rather than its speed. On the plains no predatory animals were capable of killing these great shaggy beasts. If they wandered into the foothills of the Rocky Mountains, grizzly bears and
wolves occasionally tried to feed on them, but usually even these
animals would tackle only a solitary buffalo, preferably one that
was young or old or wounded or somehow feeble. A buffalo bull
made a formidable enemy, for he usually weighed a ton, and with

his horns and hooves he could fight off most any beast. Moreover, buffalo were difficult to surprise, for while the herd grazed an old cow with an extremely good sense of smell usually stood guard. Buffalo were also good runners; once a herd stampeded, only a fast horse could keep up with them. Coronado and his men found this out to their surprise and chagrin. Writing to his king, Charles V, Coronado noted that he and his men were living almost entirely on buffalo meat but "at the cost of some of the horses slain by the cattle, for, as I told your Majesty, these animals are very wild and ferocious."[2] Because mounts were irreplaceable on the High Plains, this loss was extremely serious.

The buffalo spent their lives on the plains of the Midwest, grazing contentedly, wallowing in sand to clean themselves, drinking from and swimming in creeks and streams, and increasing in number. Calves weighed twenty-five to forty pounds at birth and were orange-red in color until about three months of age; then they assumed the dark color of the adult, a blackish or yellowish brown. By the fall after their birth, calves weighed some 400 pounds and had begun to grow the long, thick coat of wool that protected them from the wintery cold. When American pioneers first reached this region there were an estimated 5 million to 8 million buffalo in the southern herd and an equal number to the north.

Inhabiting these grasslands and river valley were a thousand varieties of small birds: killdeer, bobolink, blackbird, plover, godwit, curlew, and meadowlark. The early residents of the region sought out the birds large enough to provide food: the prairie chicken, the grouse, and the wild turkey, along with migratory ducks, geese, and other waterfowl. Wright recalled:

> It was a poor day or a poor hunter who could not kill a hundred ducks and geese in a day, and sometimes several hundred were killed in a day, so one can judge by this how plentiful they were. Then turkeys and quails—there was no end to them. Their number were countless; one could not estimate them. . . . I have seen thousands of turkeys in a flock, coming into roost on the North Fork and the main Canadian and its timbered branches.

Several times, at a distance, we mistook them for large herds of buffalo. They literally covered the prairie for miles, with their immense flocks. . . . I must not fail to mention, among our game birds, the pretty prairie plover. . . . I have often gone out and killed from one hundred to two hundred, and back to Dodge inside of four hours.[3]

Little wonder that many early immigrants to the region thought of the vicinity of Dodge as comparable to the Garden of Eden. Game flourished in many forms, water was abundant, and along the banks of the nearby river were cottonwood, elm, hackberry, ash, and box-elder trees for logs or lumber. The alluvial soil of the area was amazingly fertile and could easily be broken to the plow. There was a saying among the pioneers of the region that God, after he created the heavens and the earth, chose to make a garden for Himself and thus He designed Kansas.

The first humans to whom He gave this heaven were the Indians, nomadic wanderers who lived at the hunting and gathering stage of existence. Little about the early masters of the region is known, although anthropologists occasionally find remains of their culture. By the time Coronado came to the region, the eastern Apache subtribes dominated the area. In this environment they lived on small game, which they killed with their bows and arrows, and buffalo. This great animal provided their major supply of food; from its hides they made clothing; and from the bones they fashioned utensils. Their shelters were called tipis (tepees), portable and easily erected conical homes made of poles and buffalo hides. With the arrival of the horse, which escaped from early Spanish expeditions and multiplied on the plains, the eastern Apache became mobile, nomadic raiders, preying on their sedentary neighbors to the east: the Pawnee, the Osage, the Oto, the Kansa, the Missouri, and the Wichita.

Apache domination of the High Plains ended early in the eighteenth century with the arrival of the Comanche. Cousins of the Shoshone, the Comanche originally lived in the mountains of eastern Wyoming. With the arrival of the Spaniard and the spread of wild horses on the plains, the Comanche captured these beasts and adapted to a horse culture, becoming in a short time the world's greatest mounted warriors. Emerging from the central Rockies, they gradually moved south in search of a warmer climate and richer booty. By 1719 they had arrived at the banks of the Arkansas, across which they confronted the Apache. The two tribes soon became deadly enemies, but the Comanche almost always won the battles that occurred. By 1743 the Comanche were at San Antonio, and thereafter they raided regularly as far south as the Gulf of Mexico, occasionally raiding deep into Mexico.

. A plains tribe living on horseback, the Comanche were nomadic buffalo hunters, rarely bothering to plant or harvest crops. Their homes were tipis made of buffalo hides and lodge poles cut in the mountains. The Comanche roamed in small bands, following whatever war chief they pleased, going north during the summer and south in the winter, and taking what they wanted from anyone they encountered. Their domain was from the Texas Panhandle north to Kansas, and from the Rocky Mountains east to the edge of the timbered country. Within this vast area they were divided into a number of bands held together only by a common language and set of beliefs, which meant that during negotiations the Comanche could not be represented by one chief and that even if all the chiefs signed an agreement any warrior could feel free to break it. The most important subtribes among them were the Yamparika, or Root-eaters, who ranged in the vicinity of the Arkansas River; the Kotsoteka, or Buffalo-eaters, who lived to the south of the Arkansas; the Nokoni, or Wanderers, who occupied the land along the Red River; the Quahadi, or Antelope People, whose domain was the High Plains; and the Peneteka, or Honeyeaters, who lived in western Texas.

The Comanche saw themselves as the children of the sun, superior to all other Indians and infinitely better than Spaniards and other whites. The Comanche's word for himself was "snake"; in his sign language he indicated "Comanche" by clenching the right fist over the left breast and withdrawing it with a slithery motion

to indicate stealth. This was the greatest virtue, for the measure of
a Comanche's social, political, and economic stature was the number of horses he owned, and these he usually obtained by theft.
Thus the man who became a political chief among them, the one
who was wealthy, the one who had high social standing, had to be
as stealthy as a snake. Their entire economy was based on booty
taken during raids. Prior to the arrival of the Spaniards, these raids
were undertaken against other tribes; afterward, the raids were
against Indian and Spaniard alike.

In appearance the Comanche tended to be tall and fat. He did
not believe in individual ownership of land, buffalo, or wild horses.
All these were free to all, and one took what one needed. Horses
and women were the only things of value, and a warrior could
claim ownership of as many of either as he could capture from outsiders. The only requirement was that he had to be able to provide
sufficient food for his wives and children. Overseeing each band of
warriors was a chief. Leadership did not always descend to the
chief's oldest son; rather it went to the nearest male relative of the
chief who seemed best suited to lead the people. Anyone unhappy
with the chief could leave to join the band of another chief in
whom he had more trust.

The Comanche were a warlike people who considered themselves superior to all non-Comanche, and theirs was an economy
based on continual warfare. Torture was the lot of any adult male
they captured. In fact, the torturing of prisoners was a prime
source of entertainment for a village. The only exception to their
disdain for non-Comanche was their acceptance of the Kiowa and
Kiowa-Apache as allies. This relationship meant that the Kiowa
and Kiowa-Apache, also plains Indians who had a horse-buffalo-
raiding culture, could live in relative peace in the same area as the
implacable Comanche; in return, they supplied warriors whenever
the Comanche were engaged in some campaign that demanded
large numbers of men.[4]

Until the mid-nineteenth century these Indians continued to
dominate the High Plains. Spaniards settled to the south and

southwest of them in Texas and New Mexico, and Frenchmen and Americans pushed into northeastern Louisiana, Arkansas, and Missouri. But the plains environment seemed foreign and hostile to the few non-Indian travelers who ventured into the region. Lieutenant Zebulon Montgomery Pike, who crossed the region in 1806, commented in his journal that the region reminded him of Africa, "for I saw in my route in various places tracts of many leagues where the wind had thrown up the sand in all the fanciful forms of the ocean's rolling wave, and on which not a speck of vegetable matter existed." Americans, he thought, "will, through necessity, be constrained to limit their extent on the west to the borders of the Missouri and Mississippi, while they leave the prairies incapable of cultivation to the wandering and uncivilized aborigines of the country."

Thirteen years later Major Stephen H. Long traversed the same country as he explored the headwaters of the Arkansas River, the new boundary in the Southwest between the United States and Spanish territory. He agreed with Pike's evaluation, writing, "In regard to this extensive section of country between the Missouri River and the Rocky Mountains we do not hesitate in giving the opinion that it is almost wholly unfit for cultivation, and of course uninhabitable by a people depending upon agriculture for their subsistence."

These two reports, both published, had a strong impact on the public attitude toward the High Plains, as did Long's designation of the region on his map, "The Great American Desert." This name carried over to schoolbooks of the era and the image persisted for almost half a century. If frontiersmen did not want to settle the region to farm it, however, there were those in their ranks—called Santa Fe traders—who did need to cross the area.

This trade was opened by William Becknell, who in 1821 left Franklin, Missouri, with several mule-loads of merchandise he intended to barter to Indians for furs. That fall he arrived at the site of the present La Junta, Colorado, to find the Indians had moved south. Thinking he would find them on the headwaters of the

Canadian, Becknell moved in that direction only to meet a party of scouts from the New Mexican presidio at Santa Fe. Becknell expected to be arrested, but instead was told of Mexican independence, which brought an end to Spanish restrictions on trade with foreigners. Assured of a welcome, Becknell accompanied the scouts to the ancient pueblo-capital of New Mexico, where he sold his cotton goods and trinkets for a handsome profit. Returning to Franklin, Missouri, with specie, mules, blankets, and other items of value, Becknell found a willing audience for the news that Santa Fe would welcome American traders.

In the spring of 1822 Becknell secured credit in the amount of $5000, money he used to buy more trade merchandise, three wagons, and animals and to hire twenty-one men to accompany him. Late in May 1822 he started from Missouri, proceeded to the Big Bend of the Arkansas, down it and by the site of the future Dodge City to a point some twenty miles upriver. There he chose to cross the river, instead of proceeding up it as he had the previous year, to venture across fifty dry miles to the Cimarron River, following it for a time and then striking out to Las Vegas, New Mexico, and on to Santa Fe. Becknell reached his destination on November 16, with his three wagons still in good condition, and he sold his merchandise quickly and at favorable prices. He and his men had suffered greatly, but they succeeded in opening a wagon road that would become the main branch of the Santa Fe Trail.[5]

Four other trading parties reached Santa Fe in 1822, among them the one led by James Baird and Samuel Chambers. However, they started so late in the year that they were halted by snow when they reached the Arkansas River. There they buried their merchandise and hurried on to Santa Fe to buy mules. The site they used, about five miles from the future Dodge City, thus became known as the "Caches," and was a landmark on the trail. Another party in 1822 was led by Stephen Cooper, who exchanged his goods for 400 jacks, jennies, and mules, a quantity of beaver pelts, and a large sum of specie. Such success encouraged still more traders to go down what has been called the Turquoise Trail in

1823, and they likewise met with success. In 1824 the trade began to organize formally. Early in April that year the traders assembled at Franklin, which became the headquarters of the trade until 1827 when it shifted to Independence. Moving west to Council Grove in central Kansas, where they bordered the territory of the plains Indians, they organized in semimilitary style, adopting a constitution and electing officers. This large party of eighty-three men and twenty-four wagons encountered no difficulties, and on July 28 it reached Santa Fe. There the traders exchanged goods valued at $30,000 in Missouri for $180,000 in specie, and furs worth another $10,000.

Despite the military organization and the success that year, the continued threat of Indian raids on the trade caused Missourians to demand protection from the United States government. Senator Thomas Hart Benton of Missouri championed legislation to mark the Trail and to secure peace treaties with the plains tribes that would guarantee the traders' right of transit without molestation. Congress passed this act on March 3, 1825, along with an appropriation of $30,000. President John Quincy Adams then appointed Benjamin Reeves, Thomas Mather, and George C. Sibley as commissioners to execute this task. They left Franklin on July 4, 1825, with a party of approximately forty persons. The Trail already in use proved easy to follow because of the ruts cut into the earth by the large iron-rimmed wheels of the heavily laden wagons; the party heaped up mounds of rocks or buffalo bones along the way, reaching the Mexican border at the Arkansas on September 11. With Mexican permission, the survey was completed to Santa Fe in 1826. During the course of this work, the three commissioners met with the Osage Indians at a point that Commissioner Sibley called Council Grove. However, the Comanche, the Kiowa, and the Kiowa-Apache were not parties to the treaties granting unmolested passage to the traders.[6]

Because of the federal interest and the ready profits to be made, the traffic on the Santa Fe Trail doubled again in 1825 and was followed by heavy growth in 1826 and 1827. In 1828, however, the

plains Indians made their presence known by attacking several parties of returning traders, killing some men and driving off horses
and mules. These attacks raised a storm of protest to Washington,
accompanied by demands for military protection. In 1829 Major
Bennet Riley and four companies of infantry were assigned to accompany the annual caravan to the international boundary (the
100th meridian at its juncture with the Arkansas River), where
they halted. However, when the traders were attacked six hours
later on the Mexican side of the boundary by plains Indian raiders,
Riley led his troops into Mexican territory and saved the traders.
Then he returned to the American side and waited; when the
traders returned in October he escorted them home safely.[7]

Despite the obvious success of and demonstrated need for military protection, none was given the traders in 1830 and again they
were attacked. The following year on May 27 the great mountain
man and pathfinder Jedediah Smith was killed on the Cimarron
by Comanche raiders. Again in 1832 there were intense raids,
causing the government to assign Captain William N. Wickliff
with 150 troops to accompany the traders from Council Grove to
the Arkansas. Protection also was afforded in 1834 by Captain
Clifton Wharton and an escort of soldiers, but generally the
traders had to rely on their own strength of arms and semimilitary
organization to ward off Indian attacks.

One of the traders in the caravan of 1829 protected by Major
Bennet Riley was William Bent, a former mountain man who
realized that greater profits lay in trading than in trapping beaver.
He and his brother Charles, in partnership with Ceran St. Vrain,
decided to build a permanent trading post on the upper Arkansas
(near the site of the present La Junta, Colorado). Their fort was
completed in the spring of 1834, although they already had been
doing business there for more than a year. Thereafter many Santa
Fe traders chose not to cross the Arkansas River at the Caches to
face the dry Cimarron crossing and the wrath of plains Indians,
but to continue up the river along its north bank to Bent's Fort.
After resting there, they turned southward through Raton Pass to
Las Vegas and Santa Fe.

The Mexican War greatly increased trade along the Santa Fe Trail, especially after the conquest of New Mexico by General Stephen Watts Kearny and his Army of the West. An increase in the trade likewise brought an increase in the number of Indian raids and a corresponding rise in demands for military protection. However, the first fort erected along the Trail was more for the convenience of the Army than for the protection of traders. In April 1847, Captain Daniel P. Mann, a master teamster, led a detail of some forty teamsters to a point on the Arkansas River about eight miles west of the present Dodge City. There they constructed four log houses which were connected by log walls sixty feet long and twenty feet high. The soldiers at this tiny outpost apparently did not take their duties seriously; Lieutenant George D. Brewerton, arriving at the post during the Mexican War with a small detachment of troops, wrote of the men there:

> We halted near Mann's Fort, a little government post, or halfway depot, then garrisoned by a handful of volunteers who drank corn whiskey, consumed Uncle Sam's bacon and hard tack, drew their pay with undeviating regularity, and otherwise wore out their lives in the service of their country. In the meantime these doughty warriors dispelled their ennui by chasing buffalo, or sallying forth to scout up and down, with a general understanding that they were to quarrel with the Comanches if they could catch them—a combination of circumstances which as it requires two parties to make a bargain, occurred but seldom.[8]

Despite the small size of the post and the inadequate nature of the troops there, Santa Fe traders nevertheless welcomed this as a resting point on the Trail. There they could halt, repair their equipment, and exchange their overworked animals for stock left by a previous caravan. The purpose of the post, however, was not to help traders bound for Santa Fe; it was meant as a halfway point between Fort Leavenworth and Santa Fe for repairing wagons and replacing animals on government supply trains bound for New Mexico. During the Mexican War this traffic was large, and in 1848 the post was repaired and enlarged. With the end of the war, however, the number of government trains decreased sharply, and it was abandoned in 1850 when a new post was established nearby.

Fort Atkinson was established on August 8, 1850, about two miles west of the present Dodge City. Unlike Mann's Fort, its purpose was to chastise and contain the raiding Indians rather than to provide a resting point for government wagon trains. Commanding the troops that established the post was Lieutenant Colonel Edwin V. Sumner of the 1st Dragoons. The structures erected were made of sod and thus it was known among the troops as Fort Sod or Fort Sodom, but officially it was designated Camp Mackay in honor of Colonel Aeneas Mackay, the deputy quartermaster general who had died on May 23, 1850. Captain William Hoffman of the 6th Infantry commanded there until the post was rebuilt in June 1851 on a site adjacent to the previous post; at that time it was renamed Fort Sumner. However, on June 25, 1851, it was officially renamed Fort Atkinson to honor Colonel Henry Atkinson, who had died in 1852. Apparently the reconstructed fort was far from imposing, for Indian Agent Thomas "Brokenhand" Fitzpatrick, who visited it in 1851, described it as "a small insignificant military station, beneath the dignity of the United States, and at the mercy and forebearance of the Indians."[9]

Early in June 1853 Indian Agent Fitzpatrick was ordered by the government to return to Fort Atkinson to meet with the plains Indians and negotiate treaties with them that would guarantee the right of American transit through the region. To accomplish this he left Kansas City, Missouri, on June 20 with a wagon loaded with goods and presents for the Indians. Anticipating these presents, Comanche, Kiowa, and Kiowa-Apache, most of them women, children, and the elderly, for the warriors were away on a raid against the Pawnee, began gathering at the fort. Fitzpatrick, after a lengthy trek west, finally arrived at Atkinson on July 25, the day before the conference. An agreement was reached within a day, for the Indians were impatient to get the presents they could see on the wagon; they agreed that Americans on the Santa Fe Trail would not be molested. Afterward they were given goods and presents.

Major Robert H. Chilton, commanding Atkinson at the time, shortly reported that the Comanche and their allies had indeed moved south of the Arkansas and that travelers on the Trail were not being attacked. The result was an order to abandon the fort on September 22, 1853. It was temporarily reoccupied in June 1854, but on October 2 that year it was permanently abandoned. The buildings were destroyed to prevent their being used by Indians; one visitor commented soon afterward that all that remained at Fort Atkinson were "heaps of broken sod leveled to the ground."[10] The New Mexican legislature that year asked that the fort be regarrisoned to guard against attacks on traders traveling between New Mexico and Missouri, but the House Committee on Military Affairs turned down the request.

Although Indian attacks on travelers along the Santa Fe Trail declined after Fitzpatrick's treaty in 1853, there were repeated instances of individual violations. Sometimes the victims survived to tell their story; other times they did not. One outgrowth of these attacks was the spread of tales about buried treasure along the Santa Fe Trail, for traders under attack often were said to have dug holes in which they cached the specie they had with them. For example, a myth that lingered many years in Dodge City concerned a Mexican trader named Jesus M. Martinez who came north from his native land in 1853, bound for Missouri where he intended to make a large purchase of goods; for that purpose he had with him a quantity of silver.

Just west of where Dodge City would be located, the train of 82 wagons and 120 men was attacked by an unusually persistent group of Indian warriors. Martinez had prepared for such an attack by circling his wagons and digging trenches, so the fight was hard and long. For five days the Mexicans withstood repeated charges, but at last their ammunition was gone and on the sixth day the camp was overrun. Only one Mexican survived, Jesus M. Martinez. He waited in hiding until the Indians at last withdrew, then emerged to find a portion of the silver—twenty-one bags each containing $1000. This he carried away from the scene of death and buried. He returned on foot to Mexico where he died shortly thereafter— but not before he had told his son about the treasure. Subsequently the son came to the United States and hunted in vain for the silver. Reportedly this treasure is still in the earth awaiting a discoverer.[11]

In the years following the abandonment of Fort Atkinson, momentous events occurred in Kansas. In 1854 the Kansas-Nebraska Act gave the region the status of a Territory. Settlers poured into the eastern part of the region, some of them bringing their slaves with them, others bringing a rabid dislike of the "peculiar institution." Within a short time a small civil war was raging, and Eastern newspapers labeled the region "Bleeding Kansas." By 1861 this mindless hatred had infected the entire nation, and North and South separated to do battle.

During these years of white killing white, the Indians of the plains steadily increased their attacks, for no army stood in their way. Increasingly the frontier was aflame, especially after the discovery of gold in Colorado in 1859 which dramatically increased the number of travelers bound westward, and the number of attacks on them by Indians who saw that large masses of migrating Americans caused a decrease in the number of buffalo. By April 1862 the cries for protection by Kansans on the western frontier were loud; the *Smoky Hill and Republican Union* of Junction City, Kansas, in its edition of April 4 that year, commented:

> Our "red brethren" still show unpleasant signs of "obstropulousness." The Pawnees do nothing but steal, never do anything but steal, and never will do anything but steal. Stealing is undoubtedly their "forte"—they take to it as a hog does to a mud puddle— as Rum takes a fellow to the devil. . . . Their success is perfect— a little more so than is agreeable.

The editor of the St. Louis *Western Journal of Commerce* wrote tongue-in-cheek on July 11, 1863, that Secretary of War William

Stanton should consider drafting the plains Indians into the Army;
he noted that in the vicinity of Fort Larned were some 10,000
warriors who had demonstrated their willingness to fight by threat-
ening to capture the fort.

Stagecoaches traveling down the Santa Fe Trail during the war
repeatedly were attacked. Lonely way stations were raided so frequently that horses and mules could not be kept at them in sufficient number to keep the coaches rolling. By the summer of 1864
Indians were attacking eastward as far as Marysville, Kansas
(north of Topeka). Clearly the frontier was receding, land values
were falling, and settlers were outraged. When volunteers took
matters into their own hands, as happened in Colorado on November 29, 1864, when Colonel John Chivington attacked the
Cheyenne of Chief Black Kettle, Eastern editors lashed out at the
mistreatment of the Indian. The editor of the *Western Journal of
Commerce* was so outraged at this outcry that on October 21,
1865, he wrote, "It might straighten out the vision of some of
these cross-eyed editors to be scalped a few times. We would advise a trip across the plains as a thorough curative to all such
school girl sentiment about the savages who have visited upon the
peaceful white inhabitant of the West, all the horrors of Indian
warfare for the last eighteen months."

To combat the Indian menace on the plains, the War Department shifted men westward as the war in the East began to wind
down. Perhaps more important, the Army sent some good com-
manders westward, men such as Major General Grenville M.
Dodge who, in December 1864, was assigned command of the Department of the Missouri (which included Kansas as well as Colorado, Utah, Nebraska, Wyoming, and Montana). At last all the
plains region was unified under one military command. Dodge,
after a survey of the situation, saw his task as quieting the Indians
so that travelers crossing the region could do so in safety. As yet,
the whites were content to leave mastery of the land to the na-
tives, for no one could see any way to profit from a land of little
rainfall and much grass.

Fort Dodge and Buffalo City

Grenville Mellen Dodge had an unusual background for a Civil War general. Born April 12, 1831, at Danvers, Massachusetts, he had grown to manhood clerking in a store, working at a fruit and vegetable farm, and driving a butcher cart. These endeavors provided him with a business sense that never deserted him; simultaneously he read widely and attended school in preparation for college. After graduating from Norwich University in Vermont with a degree in science, he attended a private school, emerging with a diploma as a military and civil engineer. Briefly he worked surveying town lots in Peru, Illinois, before joining the Illinois Central Railroad to survey a route across Iowa. Settling at Council Bluffs, he operated a business there while continuing to work for the railroad.

During the Civil War, he worked first on the governor's staff, then assumed the colonelcy of the 4th Iowa Regiment, eventually rising to the rank of major general of volunteers. Duty followed in Missouri, Kentucky, Tennessee, Mississippi, Alabama, and Georgia; in 1864, while serving with William T. Sherman's forces at Atlanta, he was severely wounded in the head and forced to retire temporarily. When he returned to duty late that year, he was given

General Grenville M. Dodge. *Courtesy Kansas Historical Society.*

command of the Department of the Missouri. His major task was to bring peace with the plains tribes which, during the war, had increased their raids to the point of interrupting traffic along the Santa Fe Trail, cutting the overland telegraph, moving the frontier eastward, and making life and property unsafe in western Kansas. To accomplish this formidable task he had only two cavalry regiments, both with low morale and little discipline—and neither wishing to leave the safety of their posts.[1]

First he wanted to open the road to Fort Kearny, Nebraska, and for this task ordered one of the regiments to move there. When the officers in that regiment refused to order their men out because of the cold weather, he threatened their arrest and court martial, whereupon they took the field. During that ride north, thirteen soldiers froze to death. Then in February, after the men had been drilled into some semblance of an army, Dodge led them in the field when the temperature was ten degrees below zero and two feet of snow were on the ground. Within a short time he restored telegraph communications, and soon the stagecoaches were rolling with some degree of safety. With the northern tribes subdued by this winter campaign, Dodge turned his attention to the south.

To patrol the upper Arkansas and south to the Texas Panhandle, he sent men in that direction under the command of Brevet Major General James Hobart Ford. A native of Ohio who had moved to Colorado during the Pike's Peak rush of 1859, Ford entered the Army as the captain of an independent company of Colorado infantry on December 21, 1861. The following year he was made a major, and in 1863 he became a colonel of the 2nd Colorado Cavalry; then, on December 10, 1864, he was breveted a major general of volunteers and assigned command of the District of the Upper Arkansas, which was part of the Department of the Missouri. Ford pursued the same strategy as had worked for Dodge in the north, a strong winter campaign, and it forced the Comanche and their allies to retreat southward to the Wichita Mountains of the Indian Territory (Oklahoma).[2]

The campaign over, Ford and his troops returned to Fort Larned to wait for the end of winter and to prepare for the expected spring campaign against hostile Indians south of the Arkansas River. On March 17 Ford's scouts brought word that 2000 Comanche warriors, plus additional Kiowa and Kiowa-Apache braves, were encamped on the Cimarron. The general knew that his major problem would be supplying his men once they took the field, for they would have to ride their horses hard in order to pursue the plains warriors. When Ford relayed his thoughts to headquarters at the Department of the Missouri, General Dodge responded by ordering that a post be erected at the old site of Fort Atkinson. To aid in this task, an engineer was sent from Fort Leavenworth on March 20.[3]

Before the end of March General Ford had issued the necessary orders. Captain Henry Pearce was to take Company C of the Eleventh Kansas Cavalry and perform the task. Once at the site Captain Pearce decided that the old site of Fort Atkinson was unsuitable, for it could not be defended easily; on April 5 he chose a location six miles to the east, placing the new post twenty-two miles east of the Cimarron Crossing and seventeen miles west of Mulberry Crossing. The site was on the north bank of the Arkansas River on a narrow meadow about one-fourth of a mile wide, to the north of which was a limestone bluff rising some seventy-five feet high. Because water would be needed in case of sustained attack, the men were ordered to build the first quarters as near the river as possible. Quickly the men excavated dugouts, erected tents over these, and threw dirt earthworks around them. The fort—such as it was—bore the name Dodge. Later there was some question as to whom the name honored. Some argued that it was named for Colonel Henry Dodge of the 1st Dragoons, but General Grenville Dodge believed that soldiers angry at their hard, monotonous lot at the isolated post had named the post after him.[4]

Just after the post was established, General Ford arrived with 1200 men, many of them former Confederates who had agreed to fight Indians in the West as members of the Union Army rather than rot in Union prisons. Before these men could cross the Arkansas to do battle with the Indians, however, orders arrived for them·to stay north of the river while a federal peace commission negotiated with the Comanche, Kiowa, Kiowa-Apache, and Arapaho. Eastern editors were urging an end to wars on the Indians, and the federal government responded by sending commissioners to negotiate. Ford returned in disgust with his men to Fort Larned, there to be relieved by Brigadier General John B. Sanborn. That fall the Treaty of the Little Arkansas was concluded with the four tribes; by this they agreed to stay on reservations allotted to them; however, they were permitted to hunt between the Arkansas and the Platte. Dodge was disgusted, later writing, "The policy of the United States in dealing with the Indian problem is beyond the comprehension of any sensible man. They were treated the same as foreign nations; and while they made treaties they never carried out their part of them, breaking them whenever the trend of civilization westward interfered with them in any way."[5]

Because of the treaty, the men at Fort Dodge did not have to campaign during the summer and fall of 1865 and thus were free to build a more permanent post. In the months that followed they completed seventy sod dugouts. Each of these measured ten feet by twelve. First the soldiers dug five feet below the surface of the earth, around the walls of which they laid strips of sod another two feet in height, giving each room a seven-foot ceiling; roofs were made of cottonwood branches, brush, and canvas. Each had a door on the south side facing the river; each had a hole in the roof for ventilation and light; and each had a sod fireplace for cooking and heat. Dirt bunks lined the walls for sleeping for the two to four men assigned to each "soddy."[6]

During the summer heat of 1865 the limitations and liabilities of Fort Dodge became evident. Spring rains flooded many of the quarters, and the soil remained wet for days after each downpour as the high ground drained. Poor diet, and unsanitary conditions, brought scurvy, dysentery, diarrhea, pneumonia, and a variety of

Artist's sketch of the Sutler's Store at Fort Dodge in 1867. *Courtesy Kansas Historical Society.*

fevers. Adding to the misery was an unusually severe winter in 1865-1866; during this the troops were snowbound in their quarters and cut off from the outside world as travel along the Santa Fe Trail ceased. When spring came at last, it brought heavy rains that weakened the walls of the soddies and made everyone, officers and men alike, anxious for diversion and willing to construct new quarters.

First they built a post sutler's store. This also was of sod, and the men anticipated that from it they could buy items they wanted. Building material for the structures planned at the post proved difficult to secure, however, for the trees in the area provided only firewood and fencing, not lumber. Thus a decision was made to build with stone secured from a quarry several miles to the north. While half of the troops made scouts and patrols after

Fort Dodge in 1879. *Courtesy Kansas Historical Society.*

Indian renegades, the other half sawed limestone blocks either eighteen inches or two feet thick. Sixty teamsters were engaged in hauling these to the fort where Lieutenant George A. Hesselberger oversaw construction of a hospital, a quartermaster building, a headquarters building that included quarters for the commanding officer, and two barracks, each capable of housing fifty men and equipped with a kitchen and mess room.

Other structures erected included wooden buildings to house a blacksmithy, a carpenter's shop, a grain shed, and a bake house, while sod was used to construct a corral measuring 200 by 150 feet. In the center of the fort, surrounded by these buildings, was a parade ground measuring 100 square yards. Most of this construction was completed by late 1867 despite Indian attacks on wagon trains, quarrying parties, work details, and even the fort itself. Another major problem was desertion, which usually came in the fall when the men began to dread another monotonous winter.[7]

By 1867 Indian attacks in western Kansas, as well as in northern Texas, by the plains raiders brought renewed cries for all-out war against them by frontiersmen, matched by demands from Easterners to negotiate with the Indians and treat them kindly. That

spring General Winfield S. Hancock departed from Fort Leavenworth in March accompanied by infantry, artillery, and the 7th
Cavalry of Colonel George A. Custer. Although the Indians refused to fight such a large contingent, melting away before its
advance, Hancock did manage to destroy some of their abandoned
villages and sufficiently awe them that they asked for peace. The
result was a peace commission that met with the Comanche, Kiowa,
Kiowa-Apache, Cheyenne, and Arapaho at Medicine Lodge in
October. Satanta, a Kiowa leader, voiced the Indian complaint
when he stated, "When I go up to the river I see a camp of soldiers, and they are cutting my wood down or killing my buffalo.
I don't like that, and when I see it my heart feels like bursting
with sorrow." The council ended with yet another treaty, essen-
tially the same as that of the Little Arkansas, after which presents
were given to the Indians. Governor Samuel J. Crawford of Kansas
reflected the frontier attitude about such negotiations when he
commented, "No boxes were set apart or piled up for the white
women and children whose husbands and fathers had been killed
and scalped by the fiendish devils who were waiting for the goods
in these boxes." The Treaty of Medicine Lodge had as little effect
as previous treaties, for whites continued to move westward and
the Indians continued to fight for their homeland.[8]

In the years that followed the soldiers at Fort Dodge contributed
to the campaigns undertaken. Between wars they scouted and rode
escort for stagecoaches and wagon trains. When not in the field,
they drilled and they worked at the stone quarry, the lime kiln, the
hay fields, and the timber tracts. A recreation parlor, complete with
billiard tables and card tables, also served as a school and chapel.
Whiskey could be purchased at the post sutler's store, and drunk-
enness was a problem as the soldiers tried to forget insult and sorrow. Duty was hard, discipline was harsh, and the life was miserable in the extreme. Usually deserters tried to join a wagon train,
for a lone man on the prairie invited a quick death from the Indians; a few deserters fled during the winter and froze. Yet more
men always enlisted, received their scant training, and came west

to posts such as Fort Dodge; and the wars against the Indians continued.

In the end, however, it was not the military presence or defeat on the field of battle that reduced the Indian to accepting life on the reservation. Instead it was the discovery of a technique for tanning buffalo hides into usable leather. This development came in 1871.

Even prior to this time the buffalo was hunted to the point of a slow reduction in its numbers. The railroad crews working in the West were fed on buffalo meat, commercial hunters keeping them supplied by killing many animals every week. Moreover, the Indians killed buffalo indiscriminately; often a herd would be run over a cliff as an easy means of slaughtering them, and in the process many more animals were killed than possibly could be eaten. In addition, sportsmen came from afar to hunt the beast. Washington Irving, with several companions, hunted them in the Indian Territory in 1832, and the Grand Duke Alexis of Russia came to Hays, Kansas, in 1872 for a similar outing; he was shown how to shoot by William F. "Buffalo Bill" Cody, and he managed to down one of the beasts. And there was a small commercial market for buffalo hides which were used with the hair on as robes in sleighs and carriages and as overcoats. All attempts prior to the 1870s to tan buffalo hides into commercial leather had produced a spongy product of little value.

Despite the slaughter, which had increased steadily every year since whites ventured onto the plains, no one immediately after the Civil War thought there was any real danger of overkilling. Travelers through the region usually wrote of their vast numbers. For example, Captain Benjamin Bonneville in 1832 stated that on the north fork of the Platte River "the country seemed absolutely blackened by innumerable herds." Another traveler to the Platte, John K. Townsend, wrote of the buffalo as an "incalculable multitude." As late as 1869 a herd of buffalo in western Kansas delayed a Kansas Pacific train nine hours as it crossed the track.

One young man engaged in killing buffalo for their meat was

Shooting buffalo from the train near Dodge. *Courtesy Kansas Historical Society.*

Josiah Wright Mooar, a native of Vermont who arrived in Hays City, Kansas, in 1870 at age nineteen. After working in a woolen mill in Vermont, conducting a street car in Chicago, carpentering in Rochelle, Illinois, and working the summer wheat harvest, Mooar decided to seek his fortune in the West. Arriving in Hays, he accepted a job chopping firewood while he looked around. For his work he received two dollars a cord, and by working hard he could chop two cords a day. Soon he observed Charles Rath, an old frontiersman, shooting buffalo and hauling the meat into town. Mooar learned that buffalo meat brought three to four cents a pound, for it was regularly served in restaurants and it was shipped east. Many people had developed a taste for buffalo tongue or buffalo hams, which could be shipped fresh in the winter and cured in the summer. Some butchers in the East bought buffalo meat and then sold it as beef to unsuspecting customers who probably found it better than the meat coming from the stringy longhorns making their way north from Texas.

After several months cutting firewood, Mooar used the money

he had saved to purchase three wagons, hire four helpers to skin the animals he killed, and buy supplies. With these he became a buffalo hunter. Soon he was hunting south along the Arkansas, which brought him to Fort Dodge for the first time. During this period he paid little attention to the hide of the animals he killed; in fact, he usually did not bother to skin the animal. Mooar later recalled, "We would kill a buffalo and cut it in two, right down the middle. We would leave the hide and hair on. We shipped the hindquarters and the saddles."[9] There was a small market for buffalo hides at this time, some firms in New York City paying as much as fifteen dollars for them—but only for those already tanned in the Indian manner. This was a long, laborious process, and most such hides were secured by trade from the Indians. Moreover, such hides had to be taken in the winter when the hair was long and thick. For the dried—or flint—hides taken at other months of the year, there was no market.

Then in 1870 a hide and fur dealer in Kansas City, J. N. Du-Bois, sent some of the dried hides to Germany. There the tanners developed a process for turning the hides into usable leather. Du-Bois, upon learning this, put out word that he would buy buffalo hides from the hunters at a good price; in addition, he told them how to peg the hides for drying, flesh side up, and he offered to sell them a special poison for killing the bugs that infested and damaged the hides. Naturally other dealers in hides and furs soon began to buy buffalo skins; among them was W. Lobenstein of Leavenworth, Kansas, who became one of the most active buyers. He specialized in taking the hides from hunters, sending them east to market, and paying off when he received his money. Inasmuch as he was scrupulously honest, he soon was doing a good business. During the winter of 1871-1872, Lobenstein received an order for 500 buffalo hides from an English tanner who wished to experiment. Lobenstein passed along this request to Charles Rath who, finding the order too large to fill, asked J. Wright Mooar to help. They were to be paid $2.25 for each hide.

After Mooar delivered his share of the 500 hides to Lobenstein,

"Slaughtered for the Hides," 1874. *Courtesy Kansas Historical Society.*

he still had 57 of them left. These he sent to his brother, John Wesley Mooar, who was living in New York City, with the suggestion that he try to find a buyer. When these arrived, attracting wide attention, a tanner from Pennsylvania offered $3.50 each for them. Tests in that state showed that leather of excellent quality could be made from buffalo hides, leather suitable for use in shoes, harnesses, belts for machinery, coats, and numerous other items.

With this report was an order for an additional 2000 hides. John Wesley Mooar thereupon quit his job in New York and hurried west to join his brother, for he correctly believed that a fortune could be made in buffalo hunting.

By the time John Wesley Mooar arrived in Kansas, his brother was hunting almost exclusively along the Arkansas River Valley, for he and the other hunters found this stream ideal. It was broad and shallow, easily forded, accessible to buffalo because of its low banks, filled with game, and timbered. Also, the Arkansas was the dividing line between the northern and southern herd of buffalo, both of which roamed into the region.

Soon the Mooar brothers, Charley Rath, and other pioneer hunters were joined by hundreds of would-be killers of buffalo. In fact, by the summer of 1872 a boom developed, perhaps not of the proportions of the California or Pike's Peak gold rushes, but certainly one that saw the death of millions of buffalo in the next half-dozen years. That year many of the techniques of the trade were developed. Usually the hunter—the one doing the shooting— was the leader of the party. He hired as many men as he thought he needed to skin the buffalo he killed; a party might include as many as fifteen skinners. Normally the skinners were greenhorns who wanted to learn the business. Hunters such as Wright Mooar originally had used a Springfield .50 caliber Army rifle loaded with seventy grains of powder and a swedge ring ball. Soon, however, almost all of them switched to the .50 caliber Sharps rifle, which seemed made especially for killing buffalo. This was a large, heavy weapon made not for the saddle but for a man hunting afoot. Its killing range, 600 yards, was so great that some Indians were moved to remark that the weapon "shoots today and kills tomorrow."

When the hunter sighted a herd, he tried to approach it from downwind, for buffalo had a keen sense of smell. Once near the herd, the hunter would aim for a bull and kill it. He wanted the others to mill about rather than stampede. When the herd did mill—the hunters called this a "stand"—the hunter often could kill a dozen or more of the beasts before the others began to run. A good hunter could kill large numbers in this manner. Soon there were conflicting claims as to who had killed the most buffalo. The Dodge City *Times* on August 18, 1877, noted:

> Dickinson county has a buffalo hunter named Mr. Warnock, who has killed as high as 658 in one winter. . . . Oh, dear! what a mighty hunter! Ford county has twenty men who each have killed five times that number in one winter. The best on record, however, is that of Tom. Dixon, who killed 120 at one stand in 40 minutes, and who from the 15th of September to the 20th of October, killed 2,173 buffalo. Come on with some big hunters now, if you have any.

The hunter was the undisputed boss of his party. The men camped, moved, and worked at his will. If several hunters came upon the same herd, the first party there had initial rights; the next to arrive could have the second-best position, and so on. These hunters had to possess patience, an understanding of animal nature, a sixth sense for Indian danger, and a knowledge of survival. They were bearded and rough, their clothing stiff with dried blood, their manners and language unsuited to the drawing room. They suffered from buffalo mange, exposure, and assorted vermin. When bedbugs became too troublesome, they piled their sleeping robes atop an ant hill, stirred it with a stick to anger the insects, and waited for the ants to eat the vermin. These were hard men in a hard land filled with danger. But there was no shortage of recruits.

When experienced hunters at last came to town, they were besieged by newcomers to tell of their exploits. Facing an audience of open-mouthed, sod-shanty farmers, drifters from the East, and teen-aged lads fresh from the city, the hunters outdid one another in telling tall tales about the number of buffalo they had slaughtered. These newcomers listened to a few such tales and thought themselves sufficiently knowledgeable to enter the business. They bought a wagon, a Sharps .50 caliber rifle, ammunition, and a few supplies and set out for the open country hoping to make a fortune. More often they confronted danger.

The winter of 1872-1873 proved especially severe, blizzards howling down from the north lasted several days. One storm in December roared for eight days without letup. Experienced hunters tried to watch for such storms and take to their sod dugouts to wait until the wind died and the snow halted. If they were caught in the open, they hurried to the nearest dugout, town, or fort for safety. Robert M. Wright later recalled what it was like to be caught in the storm of December 1872. He and fellow teamsters were hauling twenty wagonloads of corn to Fort Dodge just before Christmas and had encamped five miles away at the end of a warm, pleasant day. That night the blizzard hit, and by the next morning the draw in which they had camped was filled with snow and more of it was blowing so hard they "could not see from one wagon to the other." When their small supply of wood ran out, they tried to burn the corn. That proved unsuccessful, whereupon they began to burn the wagons.

Toward the end of the second day, with the blizzard still raging, two men volunteered to make an effort to reach Fort Dodge to bring relief. After bundling up in everything they could put on, they rode out on mules. At first they tried to guide the mules, but at last they realized they were totally lost and simply gave the mules a loose rein and let them follow their instincts. After eight hours they reached the fort; each was solidly frozen to his saddle. One of them was frostbitten so severely that he had to have a leg amputated. Soldiers rode out and rescued the rest just as the storm ended. The men there were in good shape and brought in the wagons they had not burned as firewood.[10]

In these storms the hunters most usually caught in the open were the greenhorns, although a few experienced men were surprised on occasion. On December 26, 1872, the Wichita *Eagle* reported that hunters were straggling into town with frozen feet and fingers following the blizzard. Then on December 31 the paper reported that hunters had brought in the body of a man from Eldorado, Kansas, who had gone to the range to make his fortune by killing buffalo; instead he had frozen. Colonel Richard I. Dodge, who commanded Fort Dodge that winter, estimated that

more than 100 hunters froze to death that year, and the post surgeon amputated arms or legs from at least seventy hunters and
railroad workers.

One of the enduring legends of blizzards and buffalo hunters
was that wily hunters, caught in blowing snow, would kill a buffalo,
pull out its viscera, and crawl inside the body cavity to stay warm.
A few such stories claimed that the hunter crawling inside had
found himself imprisoned in the frozen carcass and died. Such
tales made good telling, but few if any seem to have great sub-
stance.[11]

Despite the danger of cold weather, far more hunters entered
the business as spring settled on the plains in 1873. A depression—
then called a panic—had wreaked havoc on the economy. Desperate men, hearing of fortunes to be made by killing and skinning
buffalo, hurried west to share in the bonanza.

Another major danger to the hunters was the Indians, who also
spread across the range each spring in search of buffalo. The
Treaty of Medicine Lodge of 1867 had guaranteed the Comanche,
Cheyenne, Arapaho, Kiowa, and Kiowa-Apache that they could
hunt north of the Indian Territory to the Arkansas River "so long
as the buffalo may range thereon, in such numbers as to justify
the chase." The government thereby promised exclusive hunting
rights south of the Arkansas to these Indians. Prior to 1870 the
hunters had largely honored this commitment, not so much from
conviction as from fear. To hunt south of the Arkansas was considered suicidal, for there were many Indians and few hunters.
Nevertheless, a few did slip across, singly or in pairs, for the hunting was especially good. Some came back rich; others were never
heard from again. After 1870 the number of hunters working south
of the Arkansas increased rapidly, especially when the price of
skins rose as leather was made from it. By 1873, as the northern
herd thinned rapidly, Wright Mooar and a friend went to Fort
Dodge to talk with the commanding officer about the Army's attitude toward hunters who broke the treaty by moving southward
across the river. "Boys," replied Colonel Dodge, "if I were a buf-

falo hunter, I would hunt where the buffalo are." In this statement
he reflected the thinking of his superiors that the best way to
control the plains tribes was to exterminate their food supply. The
result of this movement southward in violation of a treaty with
the Indians was a bitter hatred of the hunters by the plains tribes,
a hatred reciprocated by the buffalo killers.[12]

There were dangers for the hunters other than cold weather and
Indians. In the spring the unwary fellow or group that encamped
in a low place could be swept away by flood waters following a
torrential spring downpour. Another hazard, one widely feared,
was rabies. The men slept in the open or in tents, and rabid skunks
or other small animals could easily attack them. Almost everyone
who was exposed to this disease died of it; the few who lived were
generally simple-minded afterward. And there was the constant
danger of accident to men far from any kind of medical assistance.
Men riding at full tilt across the plains in pursuit of buffalo or
trying to get away from Indians frequently died or were severely
injured when a horse's hoof went into a prairie dog's hole and the
animal came crashing to earth. Guns accidentally discharged,
knives slipped, a wounded buffalo got up and gored someone—the
list of dangers was long.

A hunter was not safe even in a bunk in a sod dugout. For example a man known only as Fred was asleep in a dugout when
suddenly something broke through the roof and struck him in the
face. Thinking an Indian had burst in upon him, Fred grabbed a
butcher knife he kept under his pillow, and the two fought until
at last the intruder died. Fred emerged from the dugout shouting,
"I killed him—I cut his throat and his guts out." Friends from a
nearby dugout discovered that the intruder was a buffalo that had
tried to eat the hay used to roof Fred's dugout. One hoof apparently had crashed through to awaken Fred, who grabbed it with
one hand and his knife with the other. As the roof gradually caved
in, bringing the entire animal inside, Fred had held on to the kicking and jerking leg as he sawed away with the knife until at last
he killed the animal.[13]

Despite such dangers—which, when related in some saloon with gusto, seemed comic—so many men entered the business that the number of hides being taken soon exceeded the demand, and the price for them fell rapidly. Early in 1872 the price had soared to $3.50 for a bull buffalo hide. By September 1873 buyers were paying only eighty cents to $1.50 each depending on quality. During the winter of 1874 the price fell again, bull hides bringing $1.00, cow hides sixty cents, and calf hides only forty cents. Eventually the price stabilized at approximately $1.00 per hide. Yet only one hide of each three or four buffalo killed was usable. The others were ruined by careless or inexperienced skinners or by insect damage or by spoilage through improper drying or storage.

During this slaughter, almost all the carcasses were left to rot, for there were fewer and fewer buyers of the meat. William Blackmore, a British traveler and sportsman, commented that in 1873 just to the east of Fort Dodge along the banks of the Arkansas he found "a continual line of putrescent carcasses so that the air was rendered pestilential and offensive to the last degree. The hunters had formed a line of camps along the banks of the river and had shot down the buffalos, night and morning, as they came to drink. I counted sixty-seven carcasses in one spot covering four acres."[14]

Because so many hundreds of thousands of hides were being shipped eastward each year, the buyers needed transportation to Eastern markets. This was supplied in southwestern Kansas by the Atchison, Topeka and Santa Fe. This railroad was the brainchild of Cyrus K. Holliday, one of the founders of Topeka. In 1859, in association with businessmen in that city, he secured a charter from the Territory to build a railroad from Atchison, on the Missouri River, to Topeka. Goods came upriver to Atchison by steamboat, and a railroad delivered these quickly and cheaply to the capital. Then in 1863, after the federal government began awarding charters and land grants to such lines as the Union Pacific and the Central Pacific, Holliday and his partners secured a land grant from the national government for more than 2 million acres of land belonging to Indians—payable if rails reached the western border of Kansas by March 3, 1873.

Work proceeded with agonizing slowness, however, because

Piles of buffalo hides at Dodge in 1874. *Courtesy Kansas Historical Society.*

funds were short. The first building contract west of Topeka was not signed until the summer of 1868 and work began that November. Most of that winter was spent bridging the Kansas River. By the summer of 1869 regular service was opened to Burlingame, and in another year there was scheduled traffic to Emporia. It took another year to reach Newton. By the spring of 1872 a sense of urgency was communicated from the company's headquarters to workers in the field. Track had to reach the Colorado border by March 3, 1873, or the company would lose its land grant. With the organizational genius of Thomas J. Peter, in charge of construction, along with the engineering skills of Albert A. Robinson, track began to go down more rapidly. Soon the men were laying two miles a day, connecting the East with infant towns in central and southwestern Kansas—or creating towns as they went: Hutchinson, Peace (Sterling), Ellinwood, Great Bend, and Larned. These for the most part were little more than collections of tents and frame shacks with the usual tawdry assortment of saloons featuring gambling and raw whiskey, dance halls to provide feminine companionship for the railroad workers, and mercantile establish-

Building the Santa Fe near Dodge City, 1872. *Courtesy Kansas Historical Society.*

ments with overpriced, low-quality goods. The track layers lived in hovels of one type or another at the end-of-track towns, but most of the more pretentious buildings were portable. When the end of track progressed too far ahead of the town, the workers would tear down their huts, load the materials aboard the train, along with entire buildings, and move them forward to start or increase the size of a new town. Always a few of the merchants remained behind, hoping that the old village would prosper, farmers would come to the area, and a permanent town would result.[15]

As the tracks for the Santa Fe approached Fort Dodge, there were residents in the area thinking of forming a township company. Among thcm were Robert M. Wright, a co-owner of the post sutler's store at Fort Dodge, and Colonel Richard I. Dodge, commander of the fort. Wright had first come to the area in 1859 at the age of sixteen and had remained to work for the Barlow, Sanderson & Company which sent stagecoaches three times a week down the Santa Fe Trail. In 1866 he secured a contract to supply firewood to Fort Dodge, and the following year, in partnership with A. J. Anthony, began operating the post sutler's store. An-

The first depot for the Santa Fe in Dodge. *Courtesy Kansas Historical Society.*

thony, like Wright, had worked for Barlow, Sanderson & Company. As post sutlers, they sold many things to the soldiers, among them whiskey. When Colonel Dodge assumed command there in the spring of 1872, he was angered to find enlisted men and officers drunk on duty. That summer he ordered an end to the sale of alcoholic beverages to enlisted men. Thus both Wright and Dodge saw the need for some place away from the fort where the troopers could relax and drink.[16]

Others wanted a town there for more commercial reasons, for they foresaw the potential of the location. Much of the buffalo hunting in the Midwest and Southwest was centered there, a fort with soldiers who had money to spend was nearby, and traffic on the Santa Fe passed through. The coming of a railroad ensured a future, as did the fertile soil of the area. Thus there were merchants, army contractors, dealers in buffalo hides, and caterers to more basic human needs who were ready to see a town built near the fort.

By the time talk was circulating of forming a township company, a few buildings already had been erected west of the fort. The first structure on the site of what became Dodge City was a three-room sod dugout erected by Henry L. Sitler, a rancher, in 1871. Then in the spring of 1872, just before Santa Fe surveyors arrived, George M. Hoover arrived with a wagonload of whiskey, drove it west from the fort until he had covered just more than the five miles the military reservation extended, erected a tent around two posts of sod on which he laid a foot-wide board as a bar, and sold whiskey at twenty-five cents a shot on the morning of June 17, 1872. Almost immediately there was competition, for George W. Brown and Charley Steward hauled in lumber from Russell, Kansas, erected a building fourteen feet square, and began to sell whiskey.

As the railroad neared, still other businessmen opened establishments, intending to sell both to soldiers and railroad workers. Daniel Wolf opened a general merchandise store near a tent saloon, while nearby J. B. Edwards and George O. Smith sold groceries and general merchandise and bought buffalo hides. Other establishments included a blacksmithy, a barber shop, a restaurant, and a dance hall, all operating out of tents, as did several women who entertained an endless stream of men. Next came a large building erected by Cutler and Wiley, who were the chief contractors for grading the railroad tracks; in addition to their headquarters, the building also housed their blacksmithy, a warehouse for their supplies, and a company store for their workmen. Among their subcontractors were Bat and Ed Masterson, who later gained notoriety as "lawmen."

By July, as the railroad pushed west from Larned, several new businesses dotted what was becoming a regular street in the unnamed town. Two clerks from the sutler's store at Fort Dodge, Herman J. Fringer and A. J. Peacock, built a frame drug store, while Wright and a new partner, Charles Rath, the buffalo hunter, constructed a two-story building in which they sold general merchandise and bought buffalo hides.[17]

On August 15, a month before the Santa Fe reached the growing settlement, the townsite company came into existence. Directors of this new company included names already prominent in the area: Robert M. Wright, Richard I. Dodge, Herman J. Fringer, Henry L. Sitler, Dr. William S. Tremaine (post surgeon at Fort Dodge), Captain Edward Woale, and Lyman B. Shaw. The company issued 600 shares of stock at $10 each for a total capitalization of $6000. The intent was to sell town lots at $50 each inside the 320 acres they planned to develop. A. A. Robinson, the chief engineer of the Santa Fe Railroad, was hired to plat the proposed town; this he did, using the typical grid pattern of the day, streets running parallel to or ninety degrees from the railroad right-of-way through the center of town. The streets Robinson proposed were sufficiently wide for an eight-mule team and wagon to turn around.

The next step for the township company was to show that 100 to 200 occupants were already there for them to file for 320 acres.[18] Realizing that as yet no such number of people were there, the promoters scaled down the size of their development to eighty-seven acres. According to the provisions of the federal act pertaining to the founding of townships passed in 1867, the promoters next had to have the county judge act as trustee for their actions. This proved difficult, for there was no county judge, although there was a county.

The Seventh Legislature of the state of Kansas, which began on January 8, 1867, passed legislation that year which divided all of the unorganized western part of the state into counties. This stipulated, "The county of Ford shall be bounded as follows: Commencing where the east line of range twenty-one west intersects the fifth standard parallel, thence south to the sixth standard parallel, then west to the east line of range twenty-six west, thence north to the fifth standard parallel, thence east to the place of beginning." The county was named for General James H. Ford.

However, in the summer of 1872 Ford County as yet had not been organized and hence did not have a county judge to act as trustee for the township company. A "Memorial for the Organization of Ford County, Kansas" was filed with the state government in October 1872, asking that Governor James M. Harvey proclaim the county organized (with 600 residents) and appoint Charles Rath, J. G. McDonald, and Daniel Wolf as special county commissioners.[19] This the governor could not do, for there was insufficient proof of the number of residents claimed. Not until April 5, 1873, was such proof forthcoming, whereupon Governor Thomas A. Osborn proclaimed the county organized.

By that time the township company had circumvented the law. With no county judge available to them in Ford County, they secured the services of a probate judge in nearby Ellis County, named him "ex-officio" probate judge of Ford County, and asked him to act as their agent. On June 25, 1873, he paid at the federal land office in Wichita the $108.75 required to withdraw the desired eighty-seven acres from the public domain and transfer it to the township company. Next the judge appointed three commissioners who were to resurvey the site and apportion it to those entitled to ownership; the judge then levied an assessment on the owners to pay himself for the $108.75 entry fee and to cover his own expenses. These considerations accomplished, the judge filed the township plat at the courthouse in Hays City and gave the deed to the owners.[20]

The new town at first was called Buffalo City by its inhabitants, for it immediately boomed thanks to the trade of the buffalo hunters. With the arrival of the Santa Fe in September 1872, a boxcar serving as a temporary depot until a frame structure could be completed, the little town swarmed with hide buyers and sellers. Wright later recalled:

> Hardly had the railroad reached there, long before a depot could be built . . . , business began; and such a business! Dozens of cars a day were loaded with hides and meat, and dozens of carloads of grain, flour, and provisions arrived each day. The streets of Dodge were lined with wagons, bringing in hides and meat and getting supplies from early morning to late at night. . . . I have been to several mining camps where rich strikes had been made, but I never saw any town to equal Dodge.

However, the post office department refused to honor the request for this name, for Kansas already contained a town named Buffalo. Therefore the local residents agreed that Dodge City was a logical choice for a town near Fort Dodge that was commanded by Colonel Richard I. Dodge, a leading member of the township company.

Unfortunately for the growing little town, the basis of its prosperity was being slaughtered at a rapid pace. Hundreds of thousands of hides could not be shipped out indefinitely. In 1873 alone the Santa Fe shipped 754,529 hides to market, and other railroads transported similar numbers. After 1873 there was a steady decline in the number of buffalo killed (by 1880 the animal was virtually extinct); fewer buffalo meant fewer hunters to be outfitted and entertained, which, in turn, meant fewer profits for the merchants and other residents of Dodge City.

Moreover, the decline of the buffalo was matched by victory over the fierce plains tribes which had roamed so freely in the past —and which had to be pursued by soldiers. During the winter of 1874-1875 soldiers from Texas, New Mexico, Kansas, and the Indian Territory converged on the Texas Panhandle region under the leadership of Colonel Ranald S. Mackenzie, and fourteen battles were fought. In these the spirit of the plains tribes was broken by the summer of 1875, and Comanche, Kiowa, and Kiowa-Apache warriors began streaming into Fort Sill, Indian Territory, to surrender. Seventy-five of their chiefs were arrested, tried, and sentenced to imprisonment in Florida. The rest were confined on reservations in the Indian Territory. No longer was there any reason to roam outside the reservation, for the buffalo were gone. This permanent defeat of the plains tribes freed residents of Dodge City from the haunting fear of sudden attack, but it also meant an end to the usefulness of Fort Dodge—and the payroll for the soldiers there. Clearly the town needed some new source of income by 1876. Fortunately for the residents, the spring rains still fell, making the lush grass grow well in their region. With the buffalo gone, this freed the grass for consumption by some other animal. Also, the railroad tracks ran from Dodge City eastward to Kansas

City and Chicago to the packing plants there. Just at this time, Texas cattlemen trailing their herds north to Ellsworth for rail transport to these Eastern markets, found they needed a cattle trail further west, for the advancing farmers' frontier made Ellsworth no longer suitable. Dodge City, founded to cater to buffalo hunters and soldiers from Fort Dodge, was willing to undertake its new role as "cowboy capital of the world."

Four-legged Prosperity

Southcentral and southwestern Kansas owed much of its prosperity in the post-Civil War era to the grass that grew so well before the land was broken to the plow. Buffalo—nature's cattle—grazed the land to produce a product marketable in the East: meat and hide. From these came a boom period that lasted only a few years, and then the animals were gone, their bleached bones to become a symbol of the land. Even before these animals were killed—and the Indians confined to reservations—a new grazing animal came into Kansas to eat the grass and was transformed into profits. This was the longhorn, whose ancestry was more noble than his drovers recognized.

The longhorn was a direct descendant of the unseemly, lanky animals of Moorish ancestry that had been raised for centuries on the plains of Andalusia in southern Spain. Just a year after his initial voyage of discovery, Christopher Columbus imported these cattle into the Caribbean, and within a quarter of a century they had become commonplace throughout the islands. Then in 1521 Gregorio de Villalobos transported seven calves to the mainland of Mexico; there they prospered and increased in numbers. Conquistadors such as Coronado drove herds north with them, walking commissaries to be eaten as needed. From every herd driven north a few animals escaped, and they found the area in south Texas to their liking. Nature had endowed this region with everything a longhorn could want: the climate was mild, the grass grew tall, and predatory animals were few. Northward lay a vast grassland onto which they could expand.

The establishment of the Texas missions by Spaniards, beginning in 1716, marked the first effort to raise longhorns as domestic animals. By 1770 the ranches of Mission La Bahía del Espíritu Santo, near Goliad, were teeming with 40,000 longhorns between the Guadalupe and San Antonio Rivers. Cattle constituted the principal wealth of the missions and most of the private citizens in the province, and trail drives to market the animals were made to Louisiana and south into Coahuila.[1] Near the end of the colonial period, however, a demand for leather in other parts of the Spanish empire caused Texas cattlemen to butcher so many of their animals that the total destruction of the herds seemed imminent. Ramos Arizpe reported in 1811 that this slaughter was taking place "for the miserable sum of half a peso a head [for the hides involved]."[2]

The revolution in Mexico, lasting from 1810 to 1821, ended this slaughter, however, for the war disrupted trade and commerce, and the longhorn began to increase in numbers once again. Then came the entry of Anglo-Americans into Texas as Stephen F. Austin and others secured contracts to colonize the area. These new settlers brought few cattle because they found longhorns, although inferior, in such adequate numbers that they saw no reason to spend money importing cattle. Those cattle that were brought often succumbed to splenic fever, which quickly became known as "Texas fever" or "Spanish fever." This was a disease carried by ticks attached to the longhorns, and to which they were immune. As late as 1830 the longhorn outnumbered all other cattle in Texas by four to one.[3]

The early American settlers in Texas considered longhorns indigenous wild animals like the buffalo. They referred to them as "mustang cattle," "Spanish cattle," or simply "wild cattle." Those cattle brought by the settlers from the United States either died or quickly interbred with the longhorns. The result was an animal slightly different from the original longhorn. The color variations were almost unlimited: brindle, blue, mouse-colored, duns, browns, cream, yellow in many shades, black, white, red, and splotchy, speckled combinations. He grew slowly, reaching total maturity only in eight or ten years, although most ranchers considered him grown at age four when he weighed about 800 pounds; a veteran past ten might tip the scales at 1000 pounds. He was big at the shoulders, flat-ribbed, and thin at the hips, with bones showing in several places. His body was so long that frequently his back swayed. Packers later asserted the animal was "all legs and horns," but there was a considerable amount of beef on his large frame—although much of it was stringy and tough.

The animal's most famous feature was that from which he drew his name, his long horns. Legends increased the size of these horns to ridiculous extremes; cowboys reminiscing in old age would swear to sets of them measuring nine or ten feet from tip to tip, but the largest actually measured with accuracy were eight feet, one and three-eighths inches. The average spread of horns on the herds that moved up from Texas after the Civil War was less than four feet. Nor did these usually grow straight out from the head and curve upward at the tip; normally the left horn was regular in this pattern, but the right tended to curve downward and involute into a semicircle. For some reason never fully understood, the animal's horns grew bigger and longer in Texas than on the original animals driven northward from Mexico, and longer than those on the cattle in California and elsewhere in the American West.[4]

Cowboys declared that this wiry longhorn, despite his perversity and his independence, was the most likely animal for trail driving that nature ever produced. They contended that the long-legged animals had tougher hoofs, more endurance, and the ability to range farther without water than the cattle of improved blood— the "high grade stuff" of a later period. A natural-born rustler, the longhorn seemed to thrive on almost any plant it could get into its mouth. His long legs carried him tirelessly over great distances, and he was unaffected by heat, hunger, or the unmelodious songs of nightriders. Above all, he was capable of walking sixty miles between drinks of water. These virtues compensated in part for the distressing inability of the breed to produce quality beef.

Another important Spanish contribution to the cattle industry of the post-Civil War era was the mustang horse, which, like Spanish cattle, soon had a better hold on Texas soil than the Spaniard himself. This horse, whose bloodlines were strong as the longhorn, was descended from stock brought into Spain from North Africa by the Moors. After Spaniards brought mustangs into the Southwest on their expeditions, some of them, also like longhorns, managed to stray, multiply, and form wild herds that eventually roamed the Great Plains and Rocky Mountains.

Of scrubby appearance and slight stature, the mustang was changed by his environment. Because he was grass-fed year-round, he grew smaller in size, but what he lost in size and beauty he gained in wind and bottom. When the American cowboy first came to know him, the mustang was a wiry, fleet, untamed little brute that could run all day and still kick his rider's hat off at night. Perhaps because of his own wild nature, he seemed instinctively to understand what a cow was going to do and thus was a natural cow pony. Through selective breeding and the admixture of some imported blood, he became, in the course of time, somewhat larger and more tractable.[5]

The Spaniards provided almost all the ingredients for the open-range cattle industry except for the grass and water. In addition to the mustang and the longhorn, the hackamore (or *jaquima*) was also of Spanish origin, as were the lariat (or *la riata*), the sombrero, and the chaps (or *chaparejos*). The so-called Texas saddle, almost in its present form, was introduced into Spain by the Moors. And the Spaniards in Texas adapted or adopted other equipment: spurs with big, two-inch rowels, the bandana (or neckerchief), branding, the roundup, and even the trail drive itself, just as it was Spanish *vaqueros* (literally cow people) who perfected the techniques of handling cattle on horseback.

At the conclusion of the Texas Revolution, most Mexican

ranchers in south Texas abandoned their property—including cattle—and hurried southward to avoid the vengeance of Texans unable to distinguish between friendly and unfriendly Mexicans. In
1837 the government of the new republic declared all unbranded
cattle a part of the public domain free to those who could capture them. Impoverished Texas pioneers who provided themselves
with a good supply of branding irons and wielded them with vigor
were soon on their way to becoming cattle barons, for there were
an estimated 3 million animals roaming the brush.[6] However, this
took both skill and endurance, for the longhorns were wild, tough,
and extremely dangerous.

When a Texan did capture a herd of longhorns, he found himself with almost no market. After the close of the Mexican War
some cattlemen attempted to drive their animals to Mexico for
sale, but the effort was disastrous; the demand for beef there was
erratic, there was great anti-*yanqui* sentiment, bandits were plenti-
ful, and ranchers in northern Mexico had a surplus of cattle. The
best market developed prior to the Civil War was New Orleans,
which could be reached both overland and by water. In 1853 alone
an estimated 40,000 head of Texas cattle crossed the Nueces River
en route to New Orleans. Likewise, the California gold rush provided a new market. In the early 1850s cowboys drove thousands
of longhorns, worth $5 to $15 a head in Texas, across the desert
to California where they sold for as much as $150 apiece. The
enormous difficulties encountered on the long drive prevented this
from becoming a major market, however.

Another small but promising market developed in the frontier
towns of the Midwest, mainly in Missouri where parties westering
over the Oregon Trail outfitted. Enterprising Texans also drove
herds northward for sale to local butchers, meatpackers in Kansas
City and Chicago, and the commissary department of the United
States Army. In 1854 about 50,000 head of longhorns crossed the
Red River bound northward. But these markets were irregular and
minor, and the longhorn continued to increase in number despite
such sales. Better markets clearly were needed.

Then came the Civil War, and Texas cattlemen dropped their branding irons and took up shooting irons. The longhorn was left to fend for itself, something it did extremely well, for its numbers increased to some 5 million in Texas by 1865. Cattlemen in the state attempted to supply beef to the Confederacy, but the Union Army made that impossible. A few Texas ranchers drove cattle overland to sell for Yankee gold after the Union captured New Orleans, but despite the premium prices they received they soon halted the activity because their neighbors considered selling to Yankees as traitorous.[7] At the same time cattle in Texas were increasing in such numbers, the cities in the North were rapidly expanding in size as they industrialized during the wartime boom. The well-paid workers in these cities were hungry for meat, which was in short supply. That boom continued into the postwar period.

Texans returning from the war found their Confederate currency worthless and their economy wrecked. But they did have beef, worth only a few dollars a head, or even free to anyone willing to go out and round it up. This was beef that would bring $40 to $50 a head in Northern and Eastern markets with which Texas had no rail connections. The $4 steer needed some way to be connected to the $40 market. A few ranchers tried to reopen the market at New Orleans by shipping cattle there. However, shipping rates were too high to make this profitable; although it cost only an estimated sixty cents to raise a four-year-old marketable steer in Texas, there was little money in Louisiana and the cost of shipping was more than a cow could bring.[8]

In the spring of 1866 a few Texas ranchers drove herds of longhorns overland to Sedalia, Missouri, over what they called the Sedalia Trail (or the Shawnee Trail). They went to Sedalia because that was the nearest railhead offering them access to Eastern and Northern markets. However, that first year of the long drive was almost the last. Not yet experienced in trail driving, the cowboys found the half-wild cattle difficult to manage across the Ozark Mountains and through pine forests. Moreover, in Missouri they were confronted with anti-Southern feelings, mob violence, and lawlessness, while mobs of angry Missouri farmers, fearful that the herds would infect their own cattle with Texas fever, halted the longhorns at county lines or else shot at and stampeded them. Very few Texas drovers made money that year at Sedalia.[9]

The need to develop a better marketing place west of Missouri was an obvious step, and several individuals, companies, and towns entered the competition. The Union Pacific's Eastern Division, later to be reorganized as the Kansas Pacific, was building westward from Topeka to enter or create several small towns: Abilene, Solomon City, and Detroit. Each of these was in Dickinson County, each had rail connections, and each had aspirations for growth. The economic benefits of securing the Texas cattle trade were obvious to a few people in and near these towns, but in the county were many farmers who did not want their domestic cattle infected with splenic fever. In fact, so angry were many Kansans at this threat that the state legislature had passed a statute in 1861 forbidding the driving of longhorns into the state during the summer (during the winter the cold killed the ticks that carried the fever). To secure the cattle trade certain individuals in 1867 lobbied a bill through the legislature opening the unsettled southwestern quarter of the state to Texas cattle; moreover, it allowed Texas cattle to be shipped through the state, and it authorized incorporated and properly bonded companies to survey a cattle trail up from the open area to a railhead on the Union Pacific.

The legislator from Abilene, Charley Thompson, was aghast at this new act as it emerged for the governor's signature. The bill originally would have opened his city for the trade, but in a compromise between House and Senate the line was drawn to exclude Dickinson County and its county seat Abilene. Obviously this act would benefit the small, new town of Ellsworth which was to the west of Abilene.

However, Abilene had one asset denied Ellsworth: Joseph G. McCoy, a twenty-nine-year-old from Springfield, Illinois, who wore a goatee to hide his weak chin. Joining his two brothers in the firm

William K. McCoy and Brothers, he prospered during the Civil War by avoiding the draft to trade in livestock. After taking a trip to the railhead of the Union Pacific and talking with everyone who seemed to know something about the cattle business, McCoy saw an opportunity for large profits if he and his brothers could establish a major shipping point; the profits would come not only from cattle sales, but also from a kickback of $5 a boxcar load of cattle shipped eastward by the Union Pacific.

Initially McCoy wanted to locate this shipping point at Junction City, but he found land there too high. Next he tried Solomon City and Salina, but farmers in those areas objected strenuously to having Texas cattle nearby. Thus in June 1867 he came to terms with Charley Thompson of Abilene, a town which McCoy termed "a small, dead place, consisting of about one dozen log huts."[10] McCoy purchased 250 acres for holding and loading pens, drew plans for an office, scales, stables, hotel, barn, and bank. By August cattle could be shipped, and he sent agents south to tell drovers about his "miracle of the plains."[11] The Texans naturally were skeptical of the alluring description painted by McCoy's agents, but one of them, Dick Copeland, cautiously agreed to drive a herd to Abilene over a trail blazed by Jesse Chisholm, a half-breed Cherokee scout. Others followed Copeland, and on September 5 the first twenty carloads of longhorns left Abilene for the Chicago slaughter houses. By the end of the season some 35,000 head reached the town, and sold for less than what the railroad charged for freighting them to market.[12]

At first many farmers in the area of Abilene objected violently to McCoy's enterprise, but he requested a meeting with them to discuss all sides of the issue. While McCoy talked, Texas drovers moved among them contracting for food and feed at high prices, whereupon the leader of the farmers arose to state, "Gentlemen, if I can make any money out of this cattle trade I am not afraid of Spanish fever, but if I can't make any money out of this cattle trade then I am damned 'fraid of Spanish fever." Because he and his fellows saw they could profit also, they dropped their opposition.[13] Farmers in nearby Detroit might rail and petition the governor to enforce the state quarantine law, but neither the governor nor Dickinson County officials would do anything. Nearby Solomon City residents, hoping to profit as they saw Abilene profiting, ceased their protest when McCoy promised to pay for any domestic cattle that died of Texas fever.

n 1868 only 75,000 longhorns came to Abilene for shipment, primarily because of the low prices received for them, an average of $20 a head. When local cattle valued at $4500 died, McCoy managed to get some Texas cattlemen to levy themselves five cents a head, raising a total of $1200; to that McCoy added $3300 of his own money, and the farmers were paid. As McCoy later recalled, "The year of 1868 closed with Abilene's success as a cattle market of no mean proportions assured beyond cavil or doubt."[14]

For five years Abilene was "King of the Cowtowns." McCoy provided the stockyards, the railroad provided transportation, and Eastern cattle buyers passed out the money. By the end of the summer of 1871, however, there were town residents, the "respectable" element, who were unhappy with what they saw as the wickedness associated with catering to the baser needs of the cowboys and cattlemen. Despite the obvious economic profits, they organized to cleanse sin from the city. Joining with them were the local farmers, who had organized themselves; they likewise wanted an end to the cattle trade because splenic fever continued to kill their domestic animals. Together the two groups drafted a notice which was printed locally and sent to newspapers in Texas:

> We the undersigned, members of the Farmer's Protective Association, and officers and citizens of Dickinson County, Kansas, most respectfully request all who have contemplated driving Texas cattle to Abilene the coming season [1872] to seek some other point for shipment, as the inhabitants of Dickinson will no longer submit to the evils of the trade.[15]

Texas drovers believed the notice and took their cattle elsewhere in 1872. The effect in Abilene was startling. By the spring of 1873, four-fifths of the business establishments in the town had closed and the population was declining rapidly. In midsummer petitions circulated in the town begging the cattlemen to return, sin and all, but the Texans already had found a new outlet. .This turn of events proved most disastrous for Joseph G. McCoy and his brothers, all of whom died poor as a result.[16]

Sixty miles southwest of Abilene was Ellsworth, also with rail connections—and temporarily west of the farmers' frontier. It had prospered thanks to the payroll at nearby Fort Harker, and enterprising merchants in the city recognized the economic benefit from the cattle trade. In 1869 they had secured state passage of an act establishing a cattle trail from their city to Fort Cobb in the Indian Territory, but the trade had not come there because of plains Indians raiding in the vicinity and the welcome that Texans then were receiving in Abilene. The actions of farmers and townspeople in Abilene in 1871 opened the way for Ellsworth to receive the business in 1872, however, and they recognized their opportunity. On March 21, 1872, the editor of the Ellsworth *Reporter* wrote, "Half of Abilene will be here in two months." He was right. By June 1 there were an estimated 100,000 Texas cattle awaiting shipment at Ellsworth. A Kansas City reporter commented that summer, "As you observe I am at Ellsworth, but not the Ellsworth of last year, for it has become thoroughly revolutionized, and to-day is the Abilene of last year. This is really the cattle mart of the great West."[17]

At the same time that Ellsworth was wooing cattlemen, so also was Newton, a town that mushroomed with the arrival of the Santa Fe in 1872. Approximately 350,000 head of cattle passed through its loading pens by the end of the year. In 1873 the two towns received 405,000 Texas cattle for sale and shipment, but prices were disastrously low that panic year; at $13 a head, only about one-fourth of the cattle found buyers. One Texas firm lost $180,000 in just three weeks, for cattle were selling for little more than freight charges.[18] As a result the number of Texas longhorns coming north declined sharply in 1874 and 1875.

Meanwhile, railroads continued to lay track closer to the Texas source of longhorns. The Missouri, Kansas, and Texas Railroad reached Denison, just south of the Red River in east Texas, in 1873, bringing a rail connection into the Lone Star State, but cattlemen continued to drive their animals north to Kansas because rail transportation was more costly than trailing. Moreover, Denison was well within the farm belt where cattlemen met opposition to their longhorns and splenic fever.

Two other towns emerged briefly to vie for the cattle market: Wichita and Caldwell. Both were on the Chisholm Trail—closer to Texas than Abilene—and each had a brief day as a sales and loading point. However, both were almost instantly overrun by the farmers' frontier and the cattle drovers were choked off by rural settlement. As early as 1874-1875 officials of the Santa Fe understood the need to open a major shipping site farther west than Wichita or Caldwell. Already it had a small loading pen at Dodge City, but so few cattle had been shipped there that corporate officials paid little attention to it. By 1875 several factors combined to make Dodge extremely attractive as the major cattle shipping point for Texas cattle: the Indians at last were being confined to their reservations in the Indian Territory, the farmers' frontier had not yet reached Dodge, and the buffalo were largely gone, leaving the citizens of Dodge anxious to find another source of income for their towns. The editor of the Dodge City *Times* noted on October 14, 1876, that local citizens had "adopted wholesome measures whereby the cattle men can be treated upon general principles of equity and reciprocity." Among these were a reduction in price on "liquors, cigars, tobacco, etc., for the especial trade of the cattle men. Reductions have also been made in prices generally." To accommodate the many Texans expected, the editor noted an increase in the number of restaurants and hotels, and he said that townspeople had adopted an attitude of "live and let live," meaning that the amusements that appealed to cowboys would be tolerated.

Just as these changes were taking place in Dodge City, the Texans were pioneering the trail over which the cattle would walk.

This task was undertaken by Hige Nail, a trail boss for the Adams Brothers Cattle Company of Uvalde, Texas. Early in 1876 Nail took a herd of cattle northward across the unmarked plains far west of farmers' shacks and fields. His route was across a relatively level prairie covered by luxuriant grass and supplied by ample water in all but the driest years. He pioneered the last major cattle trail in American history, the Great Western.

This trail was born in south Texas in a triangle bounded by the cities of San Antonio, Corpus Christi, and Laredo. Brownsville was its southernmost starting point, while San Antonio and Bandera, a small town to the west, were the staging areas. From there the trail proceeded to the northwest, crossing the Red River at a point known as Doan's Store, traversed Oklahoma along or near the 99th meridian, which bounded Indian reservations, passed just west of Camp Supply, Indian Territory, entered Kansas about four miles east of the juncture of the state boundary and the Cimarron River, and terminated at the Santa Fe's stockyards a mile west of Dodge City. In the years that followed, the trail was lengthened because some cattle driven up the Great Western were not sold at Dodge; instead they continued north as far as Montana and Idaho to stock the ranges there.[19]

For a brief time after Nail opened the Great Western, there was keen competition between the towns on the Chisholm Trail and Dodge City for the cattle business. By 1879, however, the Great Western clearly dominated, and by 1885 it was the only longhorn trail in use. A major problem the cattlemen faced on this trail was complaints by Indians over whose reservation land they passed; the Indians told the Commissioner of Indian Affairs that the Texans were dawdling along, their cattle fattening themselves on grass belonging to the Indians. In 1877 Commissioner E. A. Hayt ordered that herds passing across reservation land had to travel eight to ten miles a day, that there could be no prolonged stops for grazing, and that there would be a fine of one dollar a head for any violation. However, this order could be enforced only by the soldiers at Camp Supply and Fort Sill, and there were too

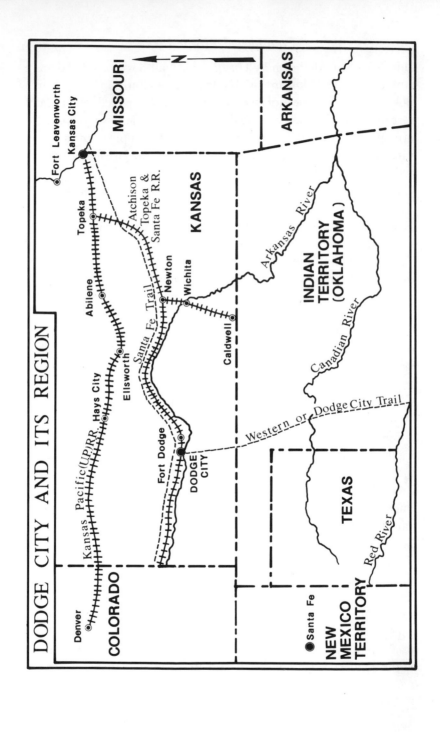

DODGE CITY AND ITS REGION

few of them to escort every herd and check on its progress. In 1878, for example, approximately 260,000 head moved north up the Great Western Trail. Occasionally an Army officer did find a herd grazing illegally, but the drover would insist that the notoriously wild longhorns had strayed or that he was encamped only for the night or that some unforeseen emergency had halted the drive. Even in those rare instances where a drover was fined a dollar a head, he paid somewhat cheerfully, for the increase in the weight of his cattle on Indian grass was worth more than the dollar-per-head penalty.[20] In 1879 local Indian Agent P. B. Hunt, with the consent of the Kiowa and Comanche leaders, decided to force cattlemen to pay for grazing privileges or face stronger regulation; most trail bosses satisfied the Indians by giving them a few of the weaker longhorns in the herd, grazing as long as they wished, and then moving on to Dodge.

Another problem faced on the Great Western Trail was increasing hostility to the movement of longhorns by ranchers trying to introduce shorthorn cattle to the Panhandle of Texas. The shorthorn was as susceptible to splenic fever as farmers' milk cows, and, when contracted, the disease was fatal in ninety-nine cases out of a hundred. Charles Goodnight, who ranched on the High Plains of west Texas, lost 975 of 1000 head because of Texas fever in 1881, and he and neighboring ranchers petitioned Governor Oran M. Roberts to quarantine longhorns in south Texas. When this failed to secure the desired result, Goodnight and his neighbors posted what was called a "Winchester Quarantine"—armed men along the edge of the Caprock with orders to shoot any longhorns driven that far west.[21]

The end of the long trail drive came for the same reason: splenic fever. The Kansas legislature passed legislation, effective March 20, 1885, which banned the importing of any Texas cattle and prohibited shipping them across the state in railroad cars. Soon other states, such as Colorado, Nebraska, Wyoming, and New Mexico, passed similar legislation.[22] This ended the day of the cattle drive—and with it the arrival each year of large numbers of

Texas cowboys in Dodge City, their pockets bulging with money and their appetites sharp for fun and excitement.

The word "cowboy," as first applied to those who worked cattle for wages, was considered a derogatory name, for those who did this task for pay were considered crude and profane men. By the 1860s, however, Texans had few qualms about entering the business as employees, for hard times made any job acceptable. And few of them needed much training, for as frontiersmen they were familiar with horses, knew how to ride and rope, were adept with firearms, and were at home in the out-of-doors. Also in that post-Civil War period came journalists from the East who wrote in glowing terms about these young men and about their environment of limpid streams, azure skies, boundless prairies, fleet-footed horses, and noble cattle. Soon almost every young lad from farm and city in the East wanted to sleep under the Western stars; they took their few possessions, wrapped them in dreams, and headed for the Southwest. Almost every train or stagecoach arriving in Texas disgorged at least one would-be cowboy. They came because they believed no other life held such romance, such glamor, such chance for glory.

Once in Texas the new cowboy wanted to dress the part. Little did he realize as he purchased these items that he was donning a costume of Spanish ancestry. The typical cowboy of that era wore heavy woolen trousers, a woolen shirt whose sleeves were held up by sleeve garters, a large hat that protected him from rain, snow, and hot sun, a neckerchief knotted around his neck to be pulled up to cover his nose in wintry cold or blowing dust, and boots that fitted well in the stirrup. Only in winter did the cowboy don a coat, for it tended to bind his arms and hold in the heat; instead he wore a vest in which he kept his watch, his tobacco, and any coins he might possess. He took great care in selecting the gloves he wore year-round, which usually were of buckskin, for they protected his hands from rope burns. His boots were a source of great pride, although he tended to be awkward in them when afoot. Finally he had chaps; made of heavy leather and fitting as a second pair of

Texas cowboys, after bathing, shaving, and dressing in their finery, pose for a photograph. *Courtesy Kansas Historical Society.*

trousers, these protected his legs against thorns and brush and were somehow a symbol of the trade to newcomers who wanted to "look like cowboys."

Because so many of these young men had read lurid tales of the cowboy life dreamed up by journalists, they also wanted a pistol to strap around their waists. In practice the weapon most often was a bother, just extra weight to be carried, for few cowboys had the money to buy the ammunition needed for practice if they were to become proficient. Gradually the newcomer learned to discard the weapon unless there was a special need for it.

Another item of great pride to cowboys was their saddle. This was designed as a place for long hours of work, so it was much like a chair but with a horn for roping. The average weight of these saddles was thirty pounds. Each cowboy was expected to provide his own saddle; thus selling it meant he was totally broke and without prospects.

Perhaps it was the long hours in the saddle that made the cowboy quiet, bottling up his emotions even among his closest friends. When he did talk, it was a salty language born from his occupation. For example, one old cowboy was asked late in life to what he attributed his longevity. He replied, "Try to get your beefsteaks three times a day, fried in taller [tallow]. Taller is mighty healing, and there's nothing like it to keep your stumich greased-up and in good working order."[23] This same life produced a raw sense of humor that appreciated the ignorance of greenhorns and the ever-present danger. Godfrey Sykes, an English immigrant who aspired to the romantic life of the cowboy, recounted that he secured his first job when an old hand became ill and could not go up the trail to Dodge City. Because he had not yet acquired his own bedroll, he was given the blankets of the sick man. In Dodge City the owner of the herd came up to Sykes and asked

about my health, and whether I had experienced any sickness on the trail. Then he told us, and both he and the trail foreman seemed to think it was rather a good joke, that the sick man whose place I had taken and whose blankets I had been sleeping in, had

been in a rather advanced stage of small-pox when he left the out-
fit. He had not thought it necessary to enquire whether I had
ever had small-pox—which I had not!—but had relied upon the
air of the plains and the bean-pot and corn-bread of our cook to
ward off infection.[24]

Once attired for the task of herding cattle and then employed
by a rancher, the cowboy found his life filled with monotony and
hard work. Cattle had to be tended, for the brutes had a knack
for getting themselves into difficulty: they had to be pulled from
quicksand, eased out of barbed wire, and dragged out of mud.
They had to be doctored and helped during calving. As barbed
wire came into widespread use, the cowboy had to build fences, a
particularly nasty job. Post holes had to be dug and wire strung.
Harness had to be kept in repair, saddles mended, and the many
types of equipment looked after. And when windmills began to dot
the landscape to provide water in the arid land, the cowboy had to
work on these monsters. In fact, on some of the bigger ranches
there was one hand whose sole job was to work on windmills.
Horses had to be broken—"gentled" was the word cowboys used—
but broken was more apt for about one in five horses had to be
almost ruined before it could be ridden, while one in a hundred
could never be ridden. Nor did the cowboy have a favorite horse
whom he loved above all other animals; that was another fiction
of the pulpsters. Because these animals were grass fed, the cowboy changed mounts frequently.

Broken bones, crippling, and death were constant threats to the
cowboy. To be thrown from a horse meant bruises at the least;
often it meant a broken leg, usually set improperly, and could be
fatal. One kick from a temperamental horse could kill, and a simple ride across the countryside could bring death if the horse was
sufficiently mean to ride deliberately under a low tree branch at
high speed. A terrified herd stampeding at night could bring injury
or death to the cowboy in a hundred ways; "stompede" was the
Texas pronunciation of a word one old-timer defined as "one jump
to their feet and another jump to hell."[25] Equally a hazard was an

unexpected blizzard in winter which could trap a cowboy on the range where he might freeze to death. Sleeping on the hard ground brought arthritis to many a cowpoke, and the simple act of roping could result in the loss of a finger or two if the hand was caught between the rope and the saddle horn. Little wonder that the average working life of a cowboy was only seven years.

Because of the shared hard work and the common danger, there was a rough equality among these young men, even for the blacks among them. Estimates of the number of black cowboys range as high as one in four; another estimate is that 5000 black cowboys helped punch cattle up the Chisholm Trail. Some of them were exslaves used by their Texas owners as workers on their ranches prior to the Civil War and kept on after emancipation; others had drifted west after the war to make a new start for themselves. In the early days of the open-range cattle era, there was little discrimination against these blacks in town or on the ranch. Some saloon-keepers required that blacks drink at one end of the bar, whites at the other end, but on the ranch black and white cowboys shared the same bunkhouse, the same hard work, the same food, even the same wages of approximately $30 a month. Only as the frontier began to close did the black cowboy find himself discriminated against in local towns.

It was for a few days in town that the cowboy lived. Because of the nature of his job, working from sunup to sundown, even at night when needed, he did not get to town every weekend. The trip most often was made about once a month at payday unless he was fortunate enough to be employed by a spread very close to a town. Once in town the cowboy most often headed for the nearest saloon where he drank too much and in the process wagered the rest of his money at gambling tables; faro, keno, and poker were his favorites, although most saloons also had a roulette table. Professional gamblers worked the cattle towns to relieve these young men of their wages, the gamblers often wearing a badge as deputy town constable to protect themselves from frequent charges of cheating.

Artist's sketch of Texas cowboys bringing longhorns to Dodge in 1878. *Courtesy Kansas Historical Society.*

An occasional cowboy drank too much and fancied himself a gunman, shooting into the air as he vented his enthusiasm. This generally brought a night in jail and a fine, for the townsmen did not want to be too rough on the cowboys for fear that they would take their business to some other frontier village. A night or a weekend in town generally sufficed for the cowboy to spend his month's wages. Then, nursing a hangover, he headed back to the ranch to get a good night's sleep, swearing that next month he would save some of his money. Somehow he never did.

Two events broke the monotony of ranch life: the roundup and the trail drive. The spring roundup was necessary to identify and brand the calves just born; always the calf was given the brand of its mother. Because this was unfenced country, all the cowboys and cattlemen in each area would come together; crews were sent into all parts of the district to drive the cattle to a central point. On the Texas range the spring roundup also was the time when the cattle to be marketed were cut out and sent north under a contract drover who guaranteed to deliver them to market, sell them at the best possible price, and take his profit in the form of a percentage.

At these roundups the cowboys were able to meet the hands from other ranches, get the gossip of their profession, hear about working conditions and wages in other parts of the country, and socialize in general. In the evening, after work ended for the day and they had eaten their fill, there was time for talk, for singing, and for telling tall tales. The cattlemen used the roundup to discuss common problems, politics, the weather, and prices at the various markets. When the roundup was completed, there usually was time for competition among the cowboys to determine who was the best rider and roper and bronc buster.

The other major event of a cowboy's life was the long trail drive. This might be to Abilene or Dodge or Ellsworth to market the cattle, or it might be all the way to Montana with stocker cattle. The typical herd sent up the trail usually numbered about 2500 animals. They were collected in south Texas at one or more ranches and turned over to the trail boss, who was known as a drover. He, in turn, employed ten to twelve cowboys to handle the herd, along with a cook and a youthful apprentice who cared for the *remuda* of a hundred or more horses.

As the herd was moved north, it stretched out into a long, sinuous line of longhorns that resembled a multicolored ribbon. Soon the animals became broken to the trail, and the daily routine became almost automatic. The trail itself, because of the passage of tens of thousands of cattle over it, was easily recognized and easily followed. Depending mainly on how well the grass was growing that year, it consisted of scores of individual, irregular cowpaths that formed a single passageway; this widened or narrowed and twisted and turned according to the terrain.

The cowboy on a drive subsisted on beans, bacon, and biscuits, fought the weather, tried to outthink the stupid longhorn, contended with bitter and resentful farmers, and confronted nature in its various forms as he attempted to deliver the animals. After two to three months on the trail, he arrived at last at Dodge City to be paid his wages. First he wanted a haircut and a shave, followed by a bath and clean clothes. Next he wanted a good meal. Clean, full, and well dressed, he then went in search of fun and adventure in saloon and brothel before departing southward for the home range. The merchants of Dodge City tried to furnish everything he might want.

The Bibulous Babylon
of the Plains

The buffalo hunters and cowboys who came to Dodge City were
not New England Pilgrim farmers in town for a Saturday of shopping, socializing, and demure fun. Colonel Richard I. Dodge,
from the vantage point of nearby Fort Dodge and several years'
experience on the frontier, wrote that the buffalo hunters were
"fearless as a Bayard, unsavory as a skunk." He saw few redeeming
virtues in those following that occupation. About cowboys he was
more generous, noting, "For fidelity to duty, for promptness and
vigor of action, for resources in difficulty, and unshaken courage
in danger, the cow-boy has no superior among men." Dodge was
no romantic, for he fully understood the "privation, hardship and
danger" that were the common lot of the cowboy; this made him
wonder "how any sane man" could voluntarily assume the life.
Perhaps it was that danger and harship, Dodge speculated, which
caused the cowboy to develop "the most ignoble of vices" and
become "the most reckless of all the reckless desperadoes developed on the frontier. Disregarding equally the rights and lives of
others, and utterly reckless with his own life; always ready with
his weapons and spoiling for a fight, he is the terror of all who

come near him, his visits to the frontier towns of Kansas and Nebraska being regarded as a calamity second only to a western tornado."[1]

The residents of communities in more settled parts of the nation would have reacted with high moral indignation had the buffalo hunter or cowboy entered their towns. They would not have wanted his business, and they would not—indeed, could not— have supplied the pleasures he sought. Dodge City was different. In the decade following 1872, Dodge was the last city on the western edge of the Great Plains, the last outpost of civilization until a traveler reached Denver. A true child of the frontier, Dodge City and its residents understood the frontiersman who made his way there. Inside its corporate limits were businessmen anxious to buy his buffalo hides or cattle and to sell him the supplies he needed to return to the plains. Moreover, there were others anxious to supply the amenities of life—a good hotel room, a barber shop, a bath, meals, and beverages—while he was in town, just as there were those in Dodge ready, for a fee, to cater to his baser needs. And finally, there were criminals ready to steal from him, even kill if necessary, to separate him from his money. Dodge was no prim, "civilized" city in the 1870s. It was a product of its environment, comfortable with the role assigned it, wide open, and ready to do business.

A correspondent for the Leavenworth *Daily Commercial*, who arrived at Fort Dodge in the summer of 1872, posted a dispatch to his editor, dated July 28, which noted the many dramatic changes taking place along the banks of the Arkansas in southwestern Kansas at that time. Little did the Indian think in 1868, wrote this correspondent, "that the scream of the locomotive would scatter the herds of his 'cattle' and drive the buffalo before it so soon. . . . Where he pitched his lodges in '67, through the energy of the officers and citizens of Fort Dodge, now has started the town of Dodge City, Kansas, which bids fair to rival Wichita —and even many of our more prominent towns." The little community was located, the reporter wrote, on the north side of the

Arkansas in the midst of bottom land which in the future would "yield crops unheard of in any portion of Kansas." It was the center of freighting south into the Indian Territory and for military posts in a vast area; it had customers in the form of soldiers at the nearby fort and buffalo hunters roaming the area; it had land that could be secured by anyone who would file on it as a homestead; and it had the Santa Fe Railroad approaching rapidly. Because of this solid economic base, the reporter believed the town had a future: "There are only a few buildings here at present, but it will improve rapidly as the track approaches—not of a mushroom growth like many of our western towns—but will steadily increase the number of inhabitants and the amount of its trade as the country develops its resources."

The Leavenworth reporter was right in his assessment, but somewhat optimistic in his description of what Dodge City was like in July 1872. Another correspondent for that newspaper reported on September 14, 1872, that the city consisted of "about a dozen frame houses and about two dozen tents, besides a few adobe [sod] houses. The town contains several stores, a gunsmith's establishment, and barber shop. Nearly every building has out the sign, in large letters, 'Saloon.' "

Three weeks later the Leavenworth *Daily Commercial* of October 5 contained a correspondent's report that "Dodge, or Buffalo City, is a hamlet containing three or four hundred souls, one drug store, tinware and gunsmith shop, a furniture and several dry goods and grocery stores, and the usual number of saloons found in all frontier towns." Growth in the town was rapid with the arrival of the railroad in September, for by the end of the year the population stood at 500. Another traveling correspondent for the *Daily Commercial* posted a story at Dodge City dated November 30, 1872, that noted that the town had "sixty or seventy buildings." Describing the business activity of the town, the correspondent wrote:

> The Government has a very extensive ware house which adds considerable to the business of the town. There is an extensive traffic

here in buffalo meat and hides, the most of which are shipped to your city [Leavenworth]. This is the terminus for the passenger trains of the A., T. & S. F. railroad at present. . . . There is a large hotel in Dodge City kept by Mr. Essington and now in good running order, although it is not quite complete. It has a capacity to accommodate about two hundred persons. There are other eating houses in the place where guests can be accommodated.

The reporter completed his story by recommending that anyone contemplating a buffalo hunt would find Dodge City an excellent place to begin, for there were thousands of the animals in that vicinity. Moreover, "All kinds of ammunition is kept in town so you need not bring supplies with you unless you choose."

From July 1872 through the following autumn, winter, and spring, Dodge City had the feel and appearance of a boom town. The businesses were housed in tents and soddies, a few frame structures gradually rising, and wagons lined the streets bringing in buffalo hides and buffalo meat and leaving with supplies and ammunition. Dozens of carloads filled with hides and buffalo meat left the freight yard by the depot each day, and dozens of carloads of grain, flour, provisions, and supplies arrived daily from the East. Charles Rath, one of the first merchants to open a general merchandise store in Dodge, sent an order that fall to Long Brothers in Kansas City for 200 cases of baking powder. The Long Brothers assumed the order was an error, believing it should have read 200 boxes of baking powder rather than 200 cases, for in all of Kansas City there were not 200 cases of baking powder to be had. At last the brothers wired Rath to ask if a mistake had been made. Back came the reply, "No; double the order." A short while later a merchant from Kansas City was in Dodge and came by Rath's store to ask about the baking powder; he was shown several carloads of flour stacked up in a warehouse and was told the baking powder was to be used to turn that into bread.[2]

By the end of 1872 the town of Dodge City was beginning to take permanent shape. Because the first businesses had established themselves along the railroad right-of-way, that became the major

Looking north across the toll bridge into Dodge City. *Courtesy Kansas Historical Society.*

dividing point in the town. Because there was a street on each side of the railroad tracks, this thoroughfare, called Front Street, was almost 100 yards wide and on occasion was referred to as "The Plaza." The major intersection was the corner of Front Street and Bridge Street. This thoroughfare was so-named because the Dodge City Bridge Company, formed in 1872, built a toll bridge across the Arkansas River that was completed in 1874 at a cost of $8000; John T. Riney was the first tollkeeper. (In 1885, with the decline of the cattle trade, local citizens grew tired of paying this toll, and the bridge was purchased by the county so it would be free.)

On each side of Front Street there were false-fronted stores by the end of 1872. When it rained, the thoroughfare became little more than a river of mud in which pedestrians sank a foot deep. Therefore the merchants built eight-foot-wide wooden sidewalks in front of their stores; these had the additional protection of wooden

Many citizens lined Front Street in 1873 for this photograph. *Courtesy Kansas Historical Society.*

awnings. During rainy weather foot-wide wooden planks were laid across the streets to help pedestrians trying to cross an intersection. Nothing kept down the dust when the street became dry, however. A horse galloping down the street, a wagon or stagecoach rolling by, or cattle driven down the street kicked up dust which the eternal winds blew onto passersby and through open windows onto people and merchandise. Little was done to correct either problem until the 20th century when asphalt paving put an end to dusty and muddy streets.

On the north side of Front Street, which residents soon came to believe was the respectable side of town, businesses stretched from the railroad depot westward for slightly more than four blocks, crossing intersections at Railroad Street, First Avenue, Bridge Street, and Third Avenue. West of Third was a residential area. Directly across from the railroad depot on the corner of Railroad and Front Streets was the Dodge House. This hotel originally was constructed by J. M. Essington and was called the Essington Hotel, but in November 1872, while he was drunk, he quarrelled with the

The Dodge House, 1874. *Courtesy Kansas Historical Society.*

hotel cook and was shot. Following his death the property was acquired by F. W. Boyd and George B. "Deacon" Cox. They added to the building until it contained thirty-eight rooms, a restaurant, a bar, and a billiard hall. Its advertisements noted that it had a "first-class laundry," the "best billiard parlor in the city," and horses "bought and sold on commission."

For several years the Dodge House was considered the finest hostelry in the city, but travelers occasionally noted that there were shortcomings. A report appeared in the Topeka *Commonwealth* July 1, 1876 stating:

> I arrived in Dodge at 3 o'clock in the morning. . . . I sought the Dodge City House, kept by my old friend G. B. Cox, who had just one bed left, and about six men came in to share it. I was careful to be the first man to register, and of course got the bed, which I proposed to share with a Lieutenant Burton of the U.S.A., provided he would find other quarters for his two bird dogs which

The Great Western Hotel, 1890. *Courtesy Kansas Historical Society.*

seemed wonderfully attached to him—by a chain and a rope. The clerk would not consent to have the dogs in the office, but after about an hour of hard work the poor lieutenant got his pups into a livery stable and came to bed. The poor fellow had dog so on the brain that he could not sleep, neither let me.

Boyd and Cox were aware that the frontier environment of Dodge City did not allow them to operate at the same level of elegance as was possible in the effete East, but they accepted their lot with humor and gave the best service possible under the circumstances.

The chief competitor of the Dodge House was the Great Western Hotel, also known as the Western House, which was owned and operated by Dr. Samuel Galland. Located on the south side of Front Street at the corner of First Avenue, the Great Western specialized in serving wild game in its dining room, which Mrs. Galland presided over; buffalo, venison, and wild turkey were regularly featured, and rooms cost $1.50 per day. Dr. Galland was one

A view of Zimmerman's hardware store in 1885. *Courtesy Kansas Historical Society.*

of the few staunch prohibitionists anywhere west of the Mississippi at that time, and served "No liquor on the premises."

Scattered along Front Street's north side were several small merchants supplying such needs as clothing, barbering, boots, saddles, and drugs. Dominating the north side of Front Street, however, were two businesses. One belonged to Frederick C. Zimmerman, who advertised at the top of his false-fronted store, "Guns, Pistols, Ammunition." Under this the sign noted, "Hardware and Tinware." Born in Prussia, Zimmerman had moved to Paris where as a young man he had become a gunsmith. Arriving in New York at age thirty-four, he worked there and in Connecticut before moving west to Laramie, Wyoming, and Kit Carson, Colorado. He arrived in Dodge City the same month as the railroad, September 1872, and opened for business in a tent. Soon he built a large frame structure; there he practiced his trade as gunsmith, sold weapons and ammunition, and added a large stock of hardware. Later he also sold lumber. Joined in Dodge by his wife and children, he fought against gambling and saloons, bought a farm and experimented with various crops, and raised alfalfa successfully. His advertising certainly did not contain understatement: he labeled his firm "the mammoth establishment of F. C. Zimmerman," and stated that it carried "the largest stock of hardware and the best selected assortment of fire-arms, ammunition, and gun fixtures in Western Kansas." At his store, he wrote, the buyer could purchase "at eastern prices, pistols, rifles and shotguns of every caliber."

The other major firm on the north side of Front Street was that established by Charles Rath in partnership with Robert M. Wright and A. J. Anthony in the summer of 1872. The store took the name Charles Rath and Company and specialized in buying buffalo hides and selling general merchandise to the hunters. Near the railroad tracks they had a hide yard where the buffalo skins they purchased were unloaded, stretched, examined for quality, and baled for shipment eastward. Rath proved extremely successful in dominating this trade, for he was active in buffalo hunting himself. Leaving Anthony and Wright to manage the store, he would set out with a wagon and a team of skinners, kill buffalo, and send back wagons as soon as they were loaded with hides and meat. In this way the business flourished. That first winter the firm shipped more than 200,000 buffalo hides east along with 200 cars filled with hind quarters and two cars filled with nothing but buffalo tongues. The hide yard nearby usually had almost 50,000 hides in it awaiting shipment.

During those early months theirs was the only supply house in town, and it was returning a healthy profit. Hundred-pound sacks of flour and cornmeal were stacked to the ceiling, each selling for double what it did in Kansas City. Nothing in the store cost less than a quarter, for money flowed freely when the buffalo hunter

Fred C. Zimmerman. *Courtesy Kansas Historical Society.*

reached town. Rath was aware that prices were even higher on the
range where the buffalo were being killed, and soon he was taking
wagons loaded with supplies onto the plains, selling the goods,
and sending in the hides taken in payment. Eventually Rath sold

Robert M. Wright. *Courtesy Kansas Historical Society.*

out his business in Dodge City to Bob Wright and moved south into Texas.

Wright also bought the interest of A. J. Anthony, who later became a county commissioner and a trustee of the Presbyterian Church. When he died at the age of eighty-nine, Anthony was remembered as one of the most temperate men to have lived through the boom years at Dodge; reportedly he had gone to bed each night before eight o'clock for more than forty consecutive years.

Wright, after he took control of the firm in 1877, made immediate and dramatic changes in the building, which had been rebuilt in brick in 1876. By this time Wright had become a cosmopolitan frontiersman; he was on friendly terms and spoke the language of soldier, buffalo hunter, and freighter, but he was equally at home with railroad officials, politicians, and Eastern businessmen. His new partner was Henry M. Beverley, who had been a salesman for Charles Rath and Company; later the two men took in Charles H. Lane as a junior partner. Wright selected his partners with care, for he realized that by 1877 business in Dodge City was changing. The buffalo hunters had been generous spenders. They arrived in town with a load of hides, sold them to one or another buyer, loaded up with supplies, and then went on the town to squander their wages. Rarely did any of them leave town with much money in their pockets. But the buffalo were disappearing by 1877, and the hunters either were moving south into Texas or finding some new occupation such as ranching or farming.

Wright foresaw that this boom was ending and that another was beginning—the Texas cattle trade. In the spring of 1877 there were several towns in Kansas with facilities to load and ship the longhorns coming north from Texas, as well as to supply the goods and entertainment desired by the drovers and cowboys. Other merchants in Dodge thought so little of this trade that the city sent out no trail agents to urge the cattlemen to come to their city. Bob Wright assumed this task almost single-handedly. Regularly he sent out his own agents to tell Texas drovers of the ease with which Dodge could handle all their business—as well as to urge them to make their purchases at Wright, Beverley and Company. Henry Beverley, himself a Texan, frequently wintered in his native state and acted as a publicity agent for Dodge City, while Wright frequently made personal trips to talk with drovers and

A view of Wright, Beverley, & Co. in 1883. *Courtesy Kansas Historical Society.*

cattlemen. In 1880 he printed a large number of circulars and sent them south, assuring Texans that the farmers' frontier had not encroached to any great extent on the facilities at Dodge: "The interests of Dodge City . . . are with the Texas drive, and public sentiment will not allow the cattle-men to be hampered and harassed by the few farmers so inclined."[3]

Beverley was a particular favorite of the Texans, one reporter noting in 1878 that he "has sold a few goods this week—perhaps eight or ten thousand dollars worth." The Texas drovers, the reporter commented, "think a heap of the 'Old Jedge'" Sam Samuels, a clerk in the store in charge of the sections containing jewelry and firearms who spoke fluent Spanish and thus was able to converse with those Mexican cowboys who ventured north. One newspaper account stated, "The Mexicans look upon Sam Samuels as their Moses in this strange land." Advertisements for the store stated that it had "the largest and fullest line of Groceries and Tobacco west of Kansas City" and stated that it carried "anything or everything from a paper of pins to a portable house, groceries, provisions for your camp, ranch or farm; clothing, hats, caps, boots and shoes, underclothing, overalls, and all kinds of furnish goods; Studebaker wagons . . . , a genuine California or Texas saddle, a nobby side saddle, a set of harness, a rifle, carbine, pistol or festive Bowie knife, camp equippage of any kind, and a full assortment of building hardware." The profits from this store approached $75,000 annually.[4]

W. N. Morphy, an editor with the Ford County *Globe* and a bitter personal enemy of Bob Wright, described the store in 1877 in glowing terms:

> Those gentlemen do an immense business and make a specialty to cater to the immense Texas trade. The jingling spur, the carved ivory-handled Colt, or the suit of velveteen, and the many, many other Texas necessaries, you here find by the gross or cord. An upstairs room, thirty by seventy-five feet, is devoted entirely to clothing and saddlery. . . . This house also does a banking business for the accommodation of its customers. Mr. John Newton, the portly and benevolent *charge de affairs* of the office, will accommodate you with five dollars or five thousand dollars, as the case may be. . . . Mr. Samuels, who has special charge of the shooting irons and jewelry stock, will entertain you in Spanish, German, Russian, or Hebrew. The assistance of Mr. Isaacson, the clothier, is demanded for *parrle vous*, while Bob, himself, has to be called on when the dusky and dirty "child of the setting sun" insists on spitting and spouting Cheyenne and Arapahoe and goes square back on the king's English. They employed over a dozen outside men to check off the wagons that were loading, and their sales were on an average of a thousand dollars a day, Sundays not excepted.[5]

By his own admission, Wright found it not uncommon to remit as much as $50,000 to banks in Leavenworth for deposit.

He sent this much money eastward because there were no banks in Dodge until 1882. That year the Bank of Dodge City opened. One of its organizers was W. H. Harris, a gambler and saloon-

STREET MAP OF DODGE CITY

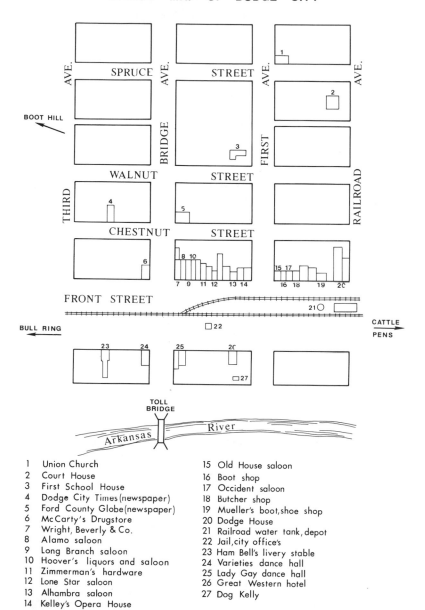

1 Union Church
2 Court House
3 First School House
4 Dodge City Times (newspaper)
5 Ford County Globe (newspaper)
6 McCarty's Drugstore
7 Wright, Beverly & Co.
8 Alamo saloon
9 Long Branch saloon
10 Hoover's liquors and saloon
11 Zimmerman's hardware
12 Lone Star saloon
13 Alhambra saloon
14 Kelley's Opera House

15 Old House saloon
16 Boot shop
17 Occident saloon
18 Butcher shop
19 Mueller's boot, shoe shop
20 Dodge House
21 Railroad water tank, depot
22 Jail, city offices
23 Ham Bell's livery stable
24 Varieties dance hall
25 Lady Gay dance hall
26 Great Western hotel
27 Dog Kelly

keeper who also bought and sold cattle. Others involved were more solid citizens. Located on the corner of Front Street and First Avenue, the Bank of Dodge City operated until 1889. Prior to the opening of this financial establishment, merchants in Dodge were expected to accept and hold large sums of money for cattlemen, who drew on these accounts as needed.

The lack of a bank in Dodge could—and did—cause trouble on occasion. One hide buyer, known as LeCompt, wandered through the streets of Dodge, his pockets bulging with cash of different denominations, waiting to buy hides. One day Wright Mooar came to town with a load of hides and began looking for Le-Compt. Mooar found the buyer at a poker table in a saloon on the south side of the tracks; somehow LeCompt had been lured into the game, and the gamblers there intended to take everything he had. Mooar, seeing what was transpiring, called LeCompt out, pretending he was in a great hurry to sell his hides and depart. With this excuse LeCompt was able to get away, later telling Mooar, "By God, you saved my life right there."[6]

The seller of hides also needed a bank in which to deposit his money. When he became drunk, as most did after selling their hides, he was an easy mark for gamblers or prostitutes. One hunter, Ed C. Jones, known as Dirty Face because he never washed, usually was very close with his money after selling his hides. He did not gamble or drink. Usually when he came to town he would stand in the back of the saloon in his dirty clothing, his feet wrapped in buffalo hide held on with wire, trying to stay warm. On one occasion, however, one of the saloon girls lured Dirty Face Jones into placing just one bet at the roulette wheel. When he won, his greed overcame his caution, and by morning he had lost $2000 in cash, his hides, his wagon, even his rifle. He never was seen in Dodge again.[7]

Across Bridge Street from Wright's store, on the north side of Front Street, was Herman J. Fringer's drugstore, which he built there in June 1872. Appointed the county clerk in 1873, he helped organize Ford County. His drugstore also served as the city post office, as well as the office for Dr. T. L. McCarty, who later purchased the drugstore and operated it as McCarty's City Drug Store. On the other side of Wright's store, just east of two saloons, was a liquor store operated by George M. Hoover and John G. McDonald. Their advertising stated, "Wholesale and Retail dealers in Foreign and Domestic Wines and Liquors. Also, the Finest Brand of Cigars." Underneath was the comment, "Pure Kentucky Bourbons, a specialty."

Finally, on the north side of Front Street adjacent to the Dodge House, was Delmonico's Restaurant, which advertised itself as the "Restaurant for the Elite." Operated by Charles Heinz, it was extremely popular as a dining room until the great fire of December 1885. Afterward it was rebuilt as both a restaurant and a hotel.

The south side of Front Street could boast little to compare with the well-known establishments across the railroad tracks. However, the south side did boast two legitimate enterprises: the Great Western Hotel, which was at the east end at the intersection with First Avenue; and Hamilton B. "Ham" Bell's Elephant Livery Stable, located at the western edge of town at the corner of Third Avenue. Bell, a native of Maryland, was a former freighter and just twenty-one years old when he arrived in Dodge in 1874. His first stable was modest in size, but in 1885 he completed a building that made his establishment the largest livery in Kansas. Freighters arriving in town knew they could leave their wagons and animals at Ham Bell's place and they would be safe. Bell, who also doubled as town mortician, was a kind man who could not turn away cowboys and transients who did not have the money to sleep in one of the hotels; he let them sleep free in the hayloft of his stable. During the height of the cattle season, as many as fifty cowboys might be found sleeping in his hayloft.

Bell, who later became a United States Deputy Marshal and a sheriff in Ford County, was best remembered for his attempt to promote good health and temperance by giving free buttermilk to anyone who would drink it. He walked the streets on occasion with a bucket of buttermilk, trying to give a dipperful to drunks.

And drunks there were aplenty, for both buffalo hunter and

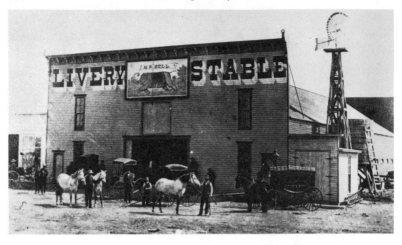

Ham Bell's Livery Stable. *Courtesy Kansas Historical Society.*

cowboy when in town tried to fill themselves full of whiskey sometimes called Forty Rod but more often Busthead. As Richard
Irving Dodge wrote about the cowboy, "His idea of enjoyment is
to fill himself full of bad whiskey, mount his mustang, tear through
the streets, whooping, yelling, flourishing and firing his pistols
until the streets are deserted and every house closed, then with a
grim smile of happiness he dashes off to his comrades to excite their
envy by graphic pictures of his own exploits and the terror of the
timid townspeople."[8]

Arriving in the city, the hunter or cowboy headed for the nearest
saloon, of which there were many. George M. Hoover became the
first merchant in Dodge when he dropped the tailgate of his
wagon five miles west of Fort Dodge on June 17, 1872, to sell
whiskey in a tent. Almost immediately he had competition from
George W. "Hoodoo" Brown, a buffalo hunter turned saloonkeeper; his establishment was the second permanent building in
the town. Another early saloonkeeper was Tom Sherman, who did
business in a frame building that featured a canvas roof and a dirt

floor. A large, lame man of mean temper, Sherman presided in rough fashion—to the sorrow of more than one hunter or cowboy. One version of the ballad, "The Streets of Laredo," contains the line, "As I walked through Tom Sherman's Barroom."⁹

In those earliest days the drinking man had only one choice when he stepped up to the bar: whiskey. And there was just one brand—the house brand. Bottled whiskey was too difficult to transport by freight wagon, so alcohol came west in barrels; this was little more than raw alcohol, which the local seller diluted, colored with coffee or caramel, flavored with black pepper, even with some dead rodent or snake to give it "body," and sold by the tumbler for twenty-five or thirty cents. After railroad tracks reached the town, bartenders and liquor dealers could purchase bottled spirits from the East. Wines, brandy, champagne, and various types of whiskey then made their appearance, along with bartenders who knew how to concoct all the latest drinks, although the favorite remained a shot of rye or bourbon. Beer likewise was unavailable until after the arrival of the railroad, for it was too bulky and inexpensive to be moved by wagon. Within a remarkably short time, the saloonkeepers of Dodge learned how to keep their beer cool in summer; temperatures in southwestern Kansas frequently exceeded the hundred-degree mark, and local citizens and transients preferred their beer chilled. To accomplish this, the saloonkeepers of Dodge built warehouses that they insulated with straw. In the winter they cut blocks of ice from the Arkansas River and stored these in the warehouses, which then cooled the beer well into the summer. When this ice melted away during the heat of summer, more ice was brought in on the Santa Fe from the mountains of Colorado.

The amount of whiskey consumed in Dodge was staggering. An article in the Dodge City *Times* in September 1878 gave one estimate:

> We don't suppose we can form an estimate of the quantity of whiskey drank in Dodge City by the number of whiskey barrels lying around loose. Morris Collar purchased one hundred empty whiskey barrels, the supposed number of barrels emptied during

the year to this date. But it would be safe to say one hundred more have been disposed of, leaving the supposed number of barrels of whiskey consumed in Dodge City in eight months at 200 barrels, or 300 barrels for one year. We don't know whether there is any credit in making this statement, and whether it reflects any credit or not, it reflects that the Bibulous Babylon keeps up its credit on a commercial commodity. The curious can estimate the number of drinks in 300 barrels of whiskey.

The term "Bibulous Babylon" was applied to Dodge by the editor of the Kinsley, Kansas, *Graphic* in an article that summer of 1878, whereupon the editor of the Dodge City *Times* used the phrase to headline an article noting the many virtues of a town it called "an oasis in the desert" and "a light house off a rocky coast." However, the editor noted that the many businesses of Dodge did alternate with saloons.

Just as they varied in atmosphere and quality, so the saloons of Dodge varied in number each year. For example, in 1877 there were sixteen of them, eight in 1878, fourteen in 1879, and thirteen in 1882. And, just as the businesses on the north side of Front Street were regarded as more respectable than those on the south side, so also were the better saloons along the north side of the street. The oldest of these was George M. Hoover's establishment. For a time he and his partner, John G. McDonald, operated a liquor store on the north side of Front Street just east of Rath and Company's general store, and they also had a tent saloon for a time on the south side of Front Street. Hoover later bought out his partner, closed the tent saloon on the south side of the street, and concentrated his efforts on his business on the north side of Front Street. His was a bar and liquor store with no dancing, no gambling, no girls, and no cards except for cribbage. In addition to whiskey and beer, he also sold cigars; in just one shipment in 1877 he received almost 5000 cigars, showing that these were a profitable item for him. After the buffalo hide business declined, Hoover welcomed the Texans, and his place became popular with them; in fact, after 1876 he began wholesaling whiskey south into the Indian Territory and the Texas Panhandle. According to his business records, his profits were high. His sales in October 1883 were $6228.67 and for October 1884 were $5523.59; these were extremely good months for him, for the fall was when many trail herds arrived. By the time Hoover sold his business in March 1885, he was known as the second largest taxpayer in Ford County (just after Bob Wright).[10]

Another longtime saloonkeeper in Dodge was A. J. Peacock. Just as the town was being established in 1872, Peacock was a clerk at the post sutler's store at Fort Dodge. Together with Herman J. Fringer, he moved to the new settlement to build a drugstore. Soon, however, he moved down the block to build a billiard parlor and saloon; at times this was called the Billiard Saloon, at other times the Main Street Saloon. His advertisements proclaimed his parlor the place for "sporting on the green," referring to the green velvet covering his billiard tables, with "round balls! and straight cues!" In addition, he stated that he took "great pride in having the very Best Brand of Wines, Liquors and Cigars." After he sold this establishment in 1876, he operated other saloons: the Lady Gay, the Nueces, and the Sample Room. However, none of these establishments attracted the "quality" patrons of some of the other saloons along Front Street.

Purchasers of the Billiard Saloon in 1876 were Chalkley M. Beeson and William H. Harris. Chalk Beeson, as he was known, had been a stagedriver in Colorado before arriving in Dodge in 1875 to collect a debt. With Harris as a partner, he changed the name of Peacock's establishment to the Saratoga, and soon they upgraded the image of the place significantly. Beeson was a skilled violinist and he provided music while Harris presided over the gambling and liquor sales. Their bartender was Adam Jackson, known locally as the "Champion Milkpunch Mixer." Their advertising stated, "This house is a first class one, conducted in the finest style and in the highest order. The proprietors take especial pains to make their customers feel comfortable."

Two years after they acquired the Saratoga, Beeson and Harris

Chalkley M. Beeson. *Courtesy Kansas Historical Society.*

sold that property and moved just west of Hoover's wholesale
liquor store to build the Long Branch. Afterward the old Saratoga
became the Lone Star Saloon and declined in reputation. The
Long Branch became one of the best establishments in Dodge,
thanks mainly to the musical talents of Chalk Beeson. Joined by

Inside the Long Branch Saloon in the 1880s. *Courtesy Kansas Historical Society.*

four other musicians—who accompanied him on another violin, a trombone, a cornet, and a piano—he and Harris advertised a five-piece orchestra that provided background music during the boom months of summer and autumn. However, no dancing or bar girls to solicit customers for prostitution were allowed. Adam Jackson followed them to the new establishment as bartender, bringing with him his reputation as the best at his trade in Dodge City. The Long Branch featured three rooms: in the front was the bar and a billiard table, along with one section reserved for the orchestra; the second room was for private gambling, for no professionals were allowed there; and the third room contained cots where drunks were put. Beeson and Harris operated the Long Branch, complete with steerhead out front to attract thirsty Texas cowboys and cattlemen, until 1883 when they sold the business, but not the building, to Luke Short.

Next door to the Long Branch, between it and Bob Wright's store, was the Alamo Saloon, which opened for business on June 1,

1877. Wright previously had used the space to provide drinks for those outfitting in his store, but under the ownership of Henry V. Cook it assumed a genteel air. The Dodge City *Times* on June 2, 1877, described the Alamo as "new and bright and quiet. It will have no music, and those who resort to its well kept parlor can hear themselves talk as well as think." Obviously this placed the Alamo in competition with the Saratoga and, later, the Long Branch where Chalk Beeson provided music. The bar of the Alamo was in the front room, while behind it was a larger area that served, according to the *Times*, as "a quiet, pleasant resort, where the cigar and refreshments can be enjoyed at leisure." Cook, "a reformed Quaker from New York," apparently was an excellent bartender, for the *Times* reported on June 17, 1877, that his "toddy (every genuine cattle man drinks toddy) increases the value of a Texas steer about $2.75."

East of these high-class establishments, near the railroad depot, was the Occident Saloon, built soon after the founding of Dodge City by Moses Waters and James Hanrahan. It, like its competitors, featured whiskey, beer, and billiards, but catered to a rougher trade than the establishments on the same block with Wright's store and Zimmerman's gun shop. Their advertising stated that Joe Miller, their bartender, would take good care of their friends and customers and that they had a "splendid livery and feed stable attached." About the time Dodge became a cattleman's town, Waters and Hanrahan sold the Occident and the stable to Henry Sturm, a German immigrant who provided good whiskey and wines, along with a dignified place in which to drink them. His advertising stated that at the Occident the customer could find "a pint, keg, or barrel of the very best, old Irish, hot Scotch, six year old hand made sour mash Kentucky copper distilled bourbon or old Holland gin," and he said he had for sale "Rhine wine sent him all the way from Alsace by his father-in-law Mr. F. Dorsheimer." There the discerning also could get Milwaukee beer and Monogram cigars, while the company was so excellent that the customer "will not go home until morning."

Sturm also featured a lunch counter where he sold sausages and cheeses. At this time Limburger was something of a novelty known for its strong smell. A local wit, learning of the Limburger and determined on a little fun, entered the Occident, placed his feet on the table, leaned back in his chair, and asked the bartender to bring him a beer, a sandwich, and some of the Limburger. When Sturm set these on the table beside his feet, the wit said that the cheese must not be good because he could not smell it. According to the account in the Dodge City *Times* on July 27, 1878, Sturm replied, "Damn it, take your feet down and give the cheese a chance."

Other saloons along the north side of Front Street included the Old House, which was part of the Dodge House, and Beatty and Kelley's restaurant and saloon. Almost all of the saloons along this street featured billiards as the chief amusement to accompany drinking, and the level of play was excellent. Jacob Schaefer, who later became a world champion player, polished his ability in Beatty and Kelley's saloon playing with Charles Ronan, a gambler.

Owning or operating a saloon on the north side of Front Street was considered a respectable occupation during these years. In fact, many of these men held positions of trust and honor in the community. John G. McDonald, George Hoover's partner, was appointed a special county commissioner by Governor Osborn when the county was organized in 1873; and Hoover became the second mayor of the city, and was a founder and charter president of the Bank of Dodge City. Moreover, George T. Hinkle, who tended bar at Hoover's saloon, defeated Bat Masterson for sheriff of Ford County in November 1879. James H. Kelley, a partner with P. L. Beatty in the saloon business, also served as mayor of Dodge City, and William H. Harris, who joined with Chalkley Beeson to operate the Saratoga and the Long Branch, was vice president of the Bank of Dodge City and city treasurer.

The saloons on the south side of Front Street were not considered respectable, however, for the amusements featured in these establishments were of a different nature. As one resident of

The Varieties Dance Hall, about 1878. *Courtesy Kansas Historical Society.*

Dodge City commented, "It was only a few steps from the Long Branch to the Lady Gay, but every step was paved with bad intentions."[11] For a time Dodge City had three establishments devoted to entertainment on the south side of Front Street. The Lady Gay, opened in April 1877 on the corner of Second Avenue, featured a built-up platform decorated with bunting for an orchestra, and was owned by Ben Springer and Jim Masterson. A year later Springer added an adjacent building which he named the Comique Theater, a name he borrowed from Harrigan and Hart's famous theater in New York City. Local citizens did not give this the French pronunciation, however; they referred to it as the Commie-cue. Another establishment on the same block was the Varieties Dance Hall, opened by Ham Bell in 1878. It was the Varieties that introduced the Can-Can to Dodge, an attraction that filled the establishment to capacity for a time. The Ford County *Globe* noted,

"The Varieties will be crowded tonight. Take a front seat, baldy, or you can-cannot see it—so well." The Varieties lasted only a short time, and was replaced by Rowdy Kate Lowe's Green Front Saloon, a notorious establishment known to cater to the lowest possible taste. For most of the boom period of Dodge City's history, however, the town had only two dance halls, one filled with white girls and patronized only by white men and the other containing black girls and patronized by both black and white men.[12]

The "hostesses" at these dance halls received part of the money paid for dancing with them—seventy-five cents for ten minutes— along with part of the cost of the drinks that their "escorts" bought for them at the bar. And most of them supplemented their income with prostitution in the bedrooms in the back of the dance hall or in their own tents and shanties usually located behind the dance hall. There was no form of medical inspection available. In fact, a common rule on the frontier was that everyone looked out for himself, a practice that contributed to rampant venereal disease among both sexes.

Thus the dance halls on the south side of Front Street featured a type of merry-making and revelry not appropriate to the sedate saloons on the north side of the street. Seemingly moral and upright men of Dodge City would drink on the north side of the street until the dark of night, when their wives went to bed, and then cross the tracks for uninhibited fun until the early morning hours. There the local residents joined in what Bob Wright characterized "the greatest abandon." Inside the buffalo hunter was dressed in blood-stained buckskins, local gentry in their Sunday best, the cattle buyer in Eastern finery, the gambler with "well-turned fingers, smooth tongue, and artistically twisted mustache," and the cowboy with Texas drawl, work-stained clothing, and spurs jingling on his boots. "Even the mayor of the city indulges in the giddy dance with the girls," wrote Wright, "and with his cigar in one corner of his mouth and his hat tilted to one side, he makes a charming looking officer."[13]

Most of these men arrived in the dance hall with a grim determination to have a good time. Local merchants and cattle buyers considered it good business to treat their prospective customers to a night of fun, while the buffalo hunter and cowboy arrived with the wages of several months' work in their pockets—and a desire to make up in a single night for all the revelry they had missed during the lonely nights on the plains. They drank the raw, potent whiskey or huge steins of beer, they smoked cigars, they talked loudly, they paid seventy-five cents to dance ten minutes with one of the dark-eyed viragoes or brazen-faced blondes, and all the while the music swirled about in loud profusion. Between dances, while the musicians rested by consuming their own share of the whiskey and beer, the "girls" escorted the men to the bar to accept a drink, which usually was tea, or they coaxed them into the back rooms.

The editor of the Dodge City *Times*, Nicholas B. Klaine, was a strait-laced Puritan who hated the sin he saw in his town, and when his paper noted the presence of these hostesses he referred to them as soiled doves, daughters of sin, fallen frails, or doves of the roost. The editors of the Ford County *Globe*, Daniel M. Frost and Lloyd Shinn, were more realistic and broad-minded, on one occasion noting that the typical dance hall consisted of "a long frame building, with a hall and bar in front and sleeping rooms in the rear. The hall was nightly used for dancing, and was frequented by prostitutes, who belonged to the house and for the benefit of it solicited the male visitors to dance. The rooms in the rear were occupied, both during the dancing hours and after, and both day and night by the women for the purpose of prostitution."[14]

Editor Klaine might refer to these girls with polite euphemisms, but in truth the business was sordid. Ham Bell, in an affidavit furnished a court in Leavenworth, Kansas, stated that he was aware of a cook who lived with her husband, fourteen-year-old daughter, and two younger children in a shanty behind one of the dance halls. The fourteen-year-old girl "carried on prostitution like the other women, and with her mother's knowledge she danced and drank as the rest." With the money she earned the young girl "helped to keep the family . . . by prostitution" as "her mother instructed and encouraged her."[15]

One visitor to Dodge in 1879 stated that in the village of 700 residents were fourteen saloons, two dance halls, and forty-seven prostitutes.[16] Few of them were "good girls gone bad," as some moralists might have claimed in that age of Victorian romanticism. Most were as crude as their customers, women such as Big Nose Kate Elder, who fought off unwanted males with a meat cleaver; Josie Armstrong, who was jealous of her sisters and pulled hair and kicked shins; and Frankie Bell, who frequently drank too much and fought anyone near her, male or female. Affidavits from the local police court reveal much of the character of these "ladies." For example, one states, "Annie Lewis of said City, being duly sworn, says that at said city, on or about the 7th day April 1877 one Sallie Doke did use indecent language toward one Annie Lewis in that the said Sallie Doke called affiant a dirty-bitch, a whore and that affiant was afflicted with the clap all of which was done in a loud and boisterous manner."

The Ford County *Globe* reported one fight between two of these girls in January 1879 under the headline "Scarlet Sluggers": "A desperate fight occurred at the boarding house of Mrs. W., on 'Tin-Pot Alley,' last Tuesday evening between two of the most fascinating doves of the roost." Describing the fight itself, the reporter noted,

> Tufts of hair, calico, snuff and gravel flew like fur in a cat fight, and before we could distinguish how the battle waned a chunk of dislocated leg grazed our ear and a cheer from the small boys announced that a battle was lost and won. The crowd separated as the vanquished virgin was carried to her parlors by two "soups." A disjointed nose, two or three internal bruises, a chawed ear and a missing eye were the only scars we could see.

Several of these girls took Southern names, just as did the saloons, knowing this would appeal to the Texas cowboys whose sentiments were Confederate. One such woman was Dixie Lee,

who, at her untimely death, left a reported $100,000 made in a
saloon in Dodge. Lawyers hunting her heirs finally found her
father, a minister in Missouri, who was extremely shocked both
by the career his daughter had chosen and the size of the fortune
she had made. A friend reportedly told the father, "It just goes to
show, Reverend, that the wages of sin are a damned sight better
than the wages of virtue."[17]

Another of these ladies was Alice Chambers. The Dodge City
Times in March 1878 noted that one day, as Alice was walking
down the street, a gust of wind blew seven dollars from her stock-
ing. "After a six-hour search participated in by all the tramps in
town, one dollar was recovered. We did suppose that the Kansas
wind was of a higher order and did not stoop to such larceny." A
few weeks later Alice lay dying at a young age—as did many of her
sisters from the whiskey they drank, the hard and depressing life
they led, and the primitive sanitary conditions under which they
lived—in a small room in the Lady Gay saloon. Reverend O. W.
Wright of the local Presbyterian Church, a newcomer in town,
visited her during the hours she lingered, whereupon he was
roundly castigated by his flock for ministering to one of the soiled
doves. She was buried in boot hill, the only woman interred there.

When business was slow in town, either because few trail herds
arrived or after the season ended, these girls always could make
money by visiting the soldiers at nearby Fort Dodge. On March 9,
1879, the *Times* noted that the commanding officer at the fort was
unhappy because of city prostitutes slipping into the enlisted
men's barracks; earlier he issued an order that "no wagons containing prostitutes are allowed to be driven through the Fort Dodge
garrison."[18]

While they worked in Dodge, these women often took false
names either to appeal to their would-be customers or to prevent
their families from finding them living lives of shame. The names
were chosen with care or were nicknames inadvertently earned:
Big Emma, Squirrel Tooth Alice, Big Nose Kate, French Mary,
Lillian Handie. Many escaped the trade through death, while

Squirrel Tooth Alice. *Courtesy Kansas Historical Society.*

others worked at it until they became sodden alcoholics. A few married hunters, cattlemen, or local citizens, but, contrary to the folklore that exprostitutes make excellent wives, several of these failed badly. For example, Lizzie Adams married George Palmer, a local rancher, but found the quiet life of a housewife on an isolated ranch unbearable. Soon she was seeing old male friends at her home in town—which suddenly burned mysteriously. Palmer was blamed for the blaze. Later he was murdered by one of Lizzie's men friends.

Beyond dancing, drinking, and prostituting, the women who worked the saloons and dance halls in Dodge City had one other duty. Where possible, when they met a cowboy, cattle buyer, buffalo hunter, or any other customer with money, they were to steer him to the gambling tables, for Dodge was a wide-open town filled with games of chance and professional gamblers. In 1878 one transient in Dodge from Pueblo, Colorado, commented, "The average Texas cow man gambles, and to supply this want almost, if not every saloon in the city, has one or more gambling tables. Faro, monte, and the other usual games are dealt openly, and most of the saloons have a private room for the votaries of draw poker."[19] The most popular forms of gambling at that time were: poker, almost always five-card draw; keno, a game similar to bingo; chuck-a-luck (or hazard), played with three dice in a wire cage shaped like an hourglass, which paid odds of 180 to 1 if all three dice showed the same number; roulette, with its thirty-six red and black numbers paying odds of 32 to 1; and faro, which had intricate rules for betting on what card would be drawn next from the pack. Those saloons featuring faro usually advertised by posting a picture of a tiger out front; thus the person who decided to gamble at faro commented that he was going to "buck the tiger," an expression that meant playing against strong odds.

Bob Wright later recorded that "Gambling ranges from a game of five-cent chuck-a-luck to a thousand-dollar poker pot. Nothing is secret, but with open doors upon the main streets, the ball rolls on uninterruptedly." Moreover, the hostesses in the dance halls would occasionally "saunter in among the roughs of the gambling houses and saloons, entering with inexplicable zest into the disgusting sport, breathing the immoral atmosphere with a gusto which I defy modern writers to explain."[20] Gambling was the most popular form of entertainment in Dodge, with professionals striving to separate the uninitiated from their money. One Ford County *Globe* reporter wrote in 1878 that, as the cattle arrived from the South, so also did the gamblers: "Just 403,901 (?) gamblers (large and small fry) are already in Dodge, prepared to help themselves to the pickings this summer."

Again in 1879 the *Globe* noted this annual influx:

> As strangers begin to congregate in the city, attracted by the approaching cattle trade, the gambler comes also; and he is more numerous this year than ever. . . . The old professional takes off his coat, arranges it on the back of his chair, and sits down in front of the faro table with as much of an air of business and composure as a bookkeeper commencing his daily labor. He bets his "system" without variation, and his countenance remains calm and immovable whether he wins or loses.
>
> The other class of gamblers are men who have other means of earning money, but who think they are just as liable to win as those more familiar with the game. They stand around the table until they think they see a card that is lucky, and immediately deposit their spare change on that card, and excitedly await developments. It is only a matter of time when their money is gone and they are left with their hands in their empty pockets, staring vacantly at the board.
>
> Then there is a class of young men who bet because they think it looks smart—boys who are not half decently dressed and who only have a few half dollars in their pockets.

Occasionally even the professionals were hoodwinked by one of their own tribe who, rather than wearing the black frock coat, string tie, and white shirt commonly identifying the breed, chose some other apparel. One man arrived dressed as a Presbyterian clergyman, saying he gambled because in such games of chance

God rewarded the virtuous and punished sinners as He chose winners and losers.When he was caught with an ace up his sleeve, he swore that it was put there by God. On another occasion a youthful farmer in old work clothes entered the Lady Gay to ask if a poker game might be in progress, saying he had a little money he wanted to venture. Quickly invited to join a game with some professionals, he then asked how to shuffle and deal—after which he won almost every hand. Later, after he had departed with the money of his opponents, the professionals learned that the green youngster was actually one of their own who adopted a rustic pose to fool everyone.[21]

Almost every major gambler of the period passed through Dodge at one time or another to try his luck at the tables. Representative of the breed was Luke Short. Born on a Texas ranch in 1854, he had traded with the Indians until he began to gamble at the mining town of Leadville, Colorado. Afterward he wandered the West as a faro dealer, gradually gaining a reputation as a gunman—a necessity for gamblers because losers often were disappointed or felt cheated and became violent. He arrived in Dodge in August 1882; local citizens could hardly believe the reputation of the man they saw, for he did not have the look of a villain. The Topeka *Journal* of May 18, 1883, described him as "a regular dandy, quite handsome, and . . . a perfect ladies man. He dresses fashionably, is particular as to his appearance, and always takes pains to look as neat as possible." Those who underestimated his abilities with a six-gun came to regret their judgment.

Another gambler of note was Robert Gilmore, called Bobby Gill in local circles. Although he participated in several street fights and was invited to move elsewhere on several occasions, he had a winning personality that made him generally well liked.

Dodge City's reputation as a wide-open town attracted many people who came solely to try their luck at gambling, to drink, and to dissipate with the girls. Bob Wright noted:

> There were numbers of people, to my certain knowledge, who would carefully save up from two hundred to five hundred dollars,

and then come to Dodge City and turn it loose, never letting up until every dollar was gone. There were others whose ambition was higher. They would save up from five hundred to two thousand dollars, come to Dodge City and spend it all. There were still others who would reach out to five thousand dollars and upwards, come to Dodge, and away it would all go, and, strange to say, these men went back to their different avocations perfectly satisfied. They had started out for a good time and had had it, and went back contented.[22]

One such man who came to Dodge with money and a thirst for fun was the exgovernor of Kansas, Thomas Carney, a wealthy merchant from Leavenworth. Arriving in March 1877, he said he was in town to purchase buffalo hides and bones for a firm in St. Louis, but actually he was there in search of a poker game with local "unsophisticated denizens." Three men, saying they were local businessmen, agreed to a friendly game with the exgovernor: Charles Norton, Robert Gilmore, and Charles Ronan, three highly skilled professional gamblers. According to a report on March 24 in the Dodge City *Times*, "The game proceeded merrily and festively for a time, until, under the bracing influence of exhilarating refreshments, the stakes were increased, and the players soon became excitedly interested." Carney at this point had a hand of four kings plus a fifth card he believed to be the ace of spades, but actually was the joker (the resemblance was close). Believing he had an unbeatable hand, he raised the ante, and was delighted when Norton raised him. As raise followed raise, the exgovernor at last threw in his watch, gold chain, and even his cuff links. Then he spread his four kings on the table, confidently expecting to rake in everything. "But at that moment a sight met the old Governor's gaze," wrote the reporter for the *Times*, "which caused his eyes to dilate with terror, a fearful tremor to seize his frame, and his vitals to almost freeze with horror." Norton calmly laid down four aces. "Slowly and reluctantly he uncoiled his arm from around the sparkling treasure; the bright joyous look faded from his eyes, leaving them gloomy and cadaverous; with a weary,

Governor Thomas Carney. *Courtesy Kansas Historical Society.*

almost painful effort he arose from the table, and, dragging his feet over the floor like balls of lead, he left the room, sadly, tearfully. . . ."

In addition to the professional gamblers, who generally ran honest games, Dodge City also had unprincipled confidence men who operated on the town plaza along the Santa Fe tracks. Their games were called "showcase games," for the operator of such a game usually had a glass showcase in which he displayed fake jewelry. When an unsuspecting cowboy stopped to purchase a trinket, he would be lured into wagering on which of three shells a pea was under or on three-card monte. Both of these games allowed easy cheating, and the cowboy enticed into such a game soon was parted from his money. The merchants of Dodge City had no objection to honest gambling—in fact, they knew it was necessary to attract cattlemen to their town; however, they constantly urged their law officers to close the showcase games, for the dishonesty involved was bad for Dodge's reputation and hurt business.

Butcher, baker, businessman, saloonkeeper, dance hall girls—all were present in Dodge City, for all were necessary to cater to the needs of the town's local population, the farmers and ranchers in the vicinity, and the many buffalo hunters and people associated with the cattle trade who came there periodically. The census of 1880 reveals that in Dodge there were twenty-one professional and technical workers, constituting 4.7 percent of the work force; sixty proprietors, managers, and officials, constituting 13.6 percent of the work force; forty-one clerical and sales people, who comprised 9.3 percent of the work force; seventy-nine craftsmen and foremen, constituting 17.9 percent of the work force; forty-two operatives, who comprised 9.5 percent of the work force; eighty-six household and service workers, constituting 19.4 percent of the work force; and 113 workers, who totaled 25.6 percent of the work force. Together these occupations totaled 442 people employed in Dodge.[23]

Yet there was more to Dodge City than the work each person performed. The people who moved to Dodge as permanent residents laughed, hoped, dreamed, looked at their children and wanted something better for them. They condoned some enterprises condemned as sinful by residents of older communities, for they knew these were necessary to their economy; however, they simultaneously erected churches and schools, formed musical and literary societies, had fraternal and civic organizations, hunted and fished, and played practical and impractical jokes. Dodge was a raw, frontier town—but one with zest and spirit that fulfilled the everyday needs of its citizens.

A Fast and Merry Town

The cowboy came to Dodge with a herd of cattle and then returned to Texas. The buffalo hunter arrived in town when he had bundles of hides and then returned to the open plains to get more. The soldier at Fort Dodge fulfilled his enlistment and then returned to his home. But for those who operated the stores, saloons, and other businesses at Dodge City, the town was home. Theirs was the task of providing the goods and services needed or desired by the cowboy, buffalo hunter, and soldier, and this they did in order to earn their livelihood. But life for them was more than making money. It involved building homes, finding wives, raising and educating children, planting trees and flowers, and laying the foundations of a permanent society—as well as escaping from the tedium of daily existence. At night the piano tinkled, the liquor flowed, and gunshots rang out, but during the day the school and church bells rang, the newspaper was printed, dentists worked on teeth, and the band practiced. A reporter from Kokomo, Indiana, was surprised during his visit in July 1878 at this aspect of life in Dodge, writing, "I was happily surprised to find the place in the daytime as quiet and orderly as a country village in Indiana."[1]

One of the great drawbacks of life in Dodge City during this period was a shortage of good women from whom the local resident

might choose a wife. In 1875 Dodge City's males outnumbered
females by a ratio of six to one; by 1880 this ratio had dropped to
three to one; as late as 1885 it stood at five to three.[2] The census
data for 1875 clearly shows a town with a large majority of its residents unmarried men in their twenties and thirties. That picture
gradually changed, but only as men went east to seek brides and
as families produced daughters who grew to marriageable age.

The first women in town were of two distinct classes: good and
bad. The bad ones were prostitutes and dance hall hostesses who
came to Dodge because it was a boom town. The good ones came
because their husbands had moved there, women such as Mrs.
Robert (Alice) Wright, who moved with her husband to western
Kansas in 1859; Mrs. Frederick C. (Matilda) Zimmerman, wife of
the gunsmith, who moved to Dodge with two babies in 1872;
Mrs. T. L. (Sally) McCarty, wife of the first doctor in Dodge,
who arrived in 1872 to keep house in a shack behind Fringer's
Drug Store; Mrs. Charles (Carrie) Rath, who came to Dodge in
1872 when her husband established his general store to purchase
buffalo hides and sell supplies; and Mrs. A. J. (Calvina) Anthony,
the daughter of a Presbyterian minister who married the post
sutler at Fort Dodge in 1872 and moved with him to Dodge that
year to raise a family of eleven children.

Calvina Anthony recorded in her diary her feelings as a bride
fresh from St. Louis when she first saw the new little town on the
plains:

> Just before our marriage the town of Dodge City was started, on
> what might be called the borders of Sahara. Very few families had
> yet shown the courage to locate in this frontier town. The morn-
> ing I arrived I looked around in vain for a woman's face, and did
> not see one until I was taken into the Dodge House and intro-
> duced to the landlady. We sat down to our breakfast with a great
> crowd of long haired hunters, with their buckskin suits and
> pistols.[3]

As more brides arrived and families grew, there were additional
good women in town, but always the young man in search of a

Mr. and Mrs. George M. Hoover. *Courtesy Kansas Historical Society.*

bride found the competition severe and his choice limited. Occasionally a family arrived with a daughter of marriageable age, or a new schoolteacher was hired from elsewhere. In 1898 the problem of finding mates was simplified by the opening of a Fred Harvey hotel and restaurant inside the Santa Fe depot at Dodge City. Harvey, working with the Santa Fe to promote tourism in the West, built a chain of quality restaurants and hotels at wayside depots. Inside the Harvey House dining room, named El Vaquero, he used only young ladies between the ages of eighteen and thirty as waitresses. Advertising in Eastern newspapers, he hired these young ladies, trained them well in social poise, and sent them west to work for $17.50 per month, plus room, board, and tips— and the opportunity to meet marrying young bachelors.

The young man in Dodge who happened to meet an eligible young woman, if he met with a smile that indicated his suit might be looked upon with favor, suddenly became addicted to bathing, to regular visits to the barber shop for a shave and a haircut, and to wearing new clothes. He resisted the local custom of "wetting down a new suit," which meant that the wearer of new clothes was supposed to celebrate the occasion by having a few drinks at a local bar, for he did not want his intended to think him a hard-drinking man. Instead he dressed in his finest, paid court to her as often as he could find an excuse, sat stiffly in a parlor chair, drank tea or coffee, attended church, and hoped somehow she would favor him above the dozen other fellows likewise suffering from tight collars, new shoes, and unfamiliar gentility. If no local girl was available, he returned for a visit to the East, married a childhood acquaintance or anyone else he found available, and brought his new bride to Dodge.

Large families were the usual practice in that age, and babies followed marriage. The first child born in Dodge was not the result of marriage, however. According to Bob Wright, a local doctor came into the drugstore one morning not long after the founding of the town and, with a look of disgust, stated, "My God! I did something last night that I never thought is possible to fall to my lot, and I am so ashamed that I never will again practice in Dodge. I delivered an illegitimate child from a notorious woman, in a house of prostitution."

Wright and the druggist were amused at the young doctor's feelings, telling him that "he must not think of leaving the profession for such a little thing as that; he must keep right on and fortune would sure follow, as it was a great field for his profession."[4] Soon afterward came the birth of Claude McCarty, son of Dr. McCarty and his wife Sally, followed by Jesse Rath, son of Charles and Carrie Rath.

Children were doubly appreciated on the frontier where few of them lived and where infant mortality rates were high. Nevertheless, in a town as unpolished as Dodge City, sentimentality did not get in the way of a good laugh—and a thumbing of the nose at convention. For example, on one occassion the Ladies Aid Society conceived the idea of a popularity contest for babies one year old or less. Votes were sold at six for twenty-five cents, each woman in the Society selling tickets to friend and stranger alike on behalf of her favorite candidate. The "good" people even went so far as to organize faro and poker games, the winnings from which were used to buy votes for one or another youngster.

When at last the evening when the winner was to be announced arrived, the Reverend O. W. Wright counted the votes and announced the winner. To everyone's surprise, the baby with the most votes was totally unknown. Nevertheless, Reverend Wright said that if the parents would bring the child forward it would receive the prize, a purse filled with gold coins. Two deacons brought forward a dove of the roost with a two-week-old baby, the winner. The gambling and saloonkeeping crowd had deliberately entered the child's name and had paid the mother $10 to be present. When an indignant woman of the congregation demanded to know the father's name, the Reverend Wright commented, "That is this lady's business," and gave her the prize. The good women were angry, but there was nothing they could do, and south of the railroad tracks the men had a good laugh.[5]

The Reverend O. W. Wright, pioneer Presbyterian minister in Dodge. *Courtesy Kansas Historical Society.*

There were swindlers who recognized the Westerner's love of children and who took advantage of his generosity. On one occasion a poor family driving a dilapidated wagon pulled by decrepit horses came to town with a sick mother and the body of a baby. They looked so pitiful that people asked questions, to which the father replied that he had no food, no clothes, even no money to bury the dead youngster. Touched, the people of Dodge quickly raised sufficient money to buy a coffin, bury the baby, provide food for the family, and give the mother a tidy sum of cash. The family then left town, but returned that night to dig up the baby—which was made of wax—and take it to the next town to play the same trick.[6]

Dodge City had a reputation for wickedness and sin, but there were Christians combating the evil and working to bring godliness to the plains. Shortly after the birth of the town it was visited by itinerant ministers who held revivals wherever they could gather a crowd. Sometimes this was done in a tent, other times in a saloon or even a dance hall. Such men had to have a strong sense of conviction, a stout heart, a willingness to endure poverty, and the ability to withstand the rough sense of humor of the area. Most of these evangelists preached against drinking, gambling, and prostitution, the livelihood of the saloon crowd, but the townspeople rarely condemned the sincerely religious person unless he intruded too heavily on them. Then they were rough, or turned the tables through humor.

One such event happened when Dodge was young. An evangelist calling himself Brother Johnson arrived and used all his magnetic power to end sin in the city. His crowds were so large that he persuaded Kate Lowe to allow him to use the Green Front Saloon as a meeting place, and every night it was filled to capacity as he pulled live snakes out of a whiskey bottle to prove the evil of such drink. Not satisfied with such success, however, Brother Johnson conceived the idea of converting Dave Mather, also known as Mysterious Dave, who at the time was city marshall and a known killer of several men. Soon Brother Johnson was out early every morning to exhort Mysterious Dave to come to the revival. Eventually, either because he wanted to placate the revivalist or he felt the tug of Christianity, Mysterious Dave agreed to come one evening. Inasmuch as Dave Mather was known to keep his word, the crowd that night was especially large, the most openly Christian members of the community in visible attendance.

When Mysterious Dave arrived, he was escorted to the seat of honor in front of the podium. Brother Johnson preached directly at Dave, his sermon filled with quotations from the scriptures about the horrors of hell and the beauties of heaven and how the angels in heaven would rejoice at the conversion of such a man as Dave Mather. Brother Johnson concluded that he knew he would go straight to heaven if he could convert such a sinner as Mysterious Dave and that he would be ready to die if he could accomplish that. When he finished, several male members of the faithful jumped to their feet to agree that they also would be willing to die and go straight to heaven rejoicing together.

During all this Mysterious Dave sat with head bowed. Later he declared that never in his life had he sweated so much, for he knew that every eye in the house was on him. He swore that he would rather have had to fight a dozen angry men armed with six-guns than that crowd of Christians. At last, however, he rose to his feet and said that he had been touched, that he was filled with religion, that he knew that if he died he would go straight to heaven. Pulling his gun, he said he was afraid that if he continued to live he might backslide and miss eternal bliss, as might the preacher and many of the congregation. Therefore he proposed to kill them right then, along with himself, in order that all might enter eternal glory. "I will send you first," he said to the preacher as he fired just above the minister's head. Then he turned and fired several shots over the heads of the faithful. All of them fell to the floor, trembling with fear, whereupon Mysterious Dave shot out the lights and walked toward the door, remarking, "You are all a set of liars and frauds, you don't want to go to heaven with me at all." The evangelist soon left the town, while the "faithful" in the congregation, after everyone laughed at them for awhile, soon backslid and returned to their sinful ways.[7]

On another occasion an itinerant preacher arrived in town to find a crowd gathered in the street. When he rode closer to see what was happening, a boy of mischievous bent rubbed bisulphite of carbon on the horse. This chemical, known locally as hokey-pokey, had the same effect as rubbing turpentine on a sore spot;

Mysterious Dave Mather, wearing a hatband proclaiming him an assistant marshal. *Courtesy Kansas Historical Society.*

it drove the animal crazy, causing it to twist and pitch and buck in an effort to rid itself of the pain. The preacher's horse reacted in typical fashion, kicking, jumping, and squalling. The preacher's hat was thrown, then his saddlebags, and then his body. Picking himself up and brushing away the dirt, he asserted, "Some ungodly person has done something to my horse." This brought gales of laughter—and the preacher's early departure from town.[8]

Despite such setbacks, the majority of the early permanent settlers of Dodge, like most frontiersmen, had a deep religious faith and wanted ministers and churches in their community. By 1876 a nondenominational church building had been erected for use by visiting clergymen. Then in February 1877 a Union Church was organized to hold services in this building, although other denominations used it still. All residents of the town, even those normally shunned by church people during regular working hours, were received in the church. However, most men of the church-going element thought nothing of taking a few drinks on Sunday morning before attending church, and afterward stopping by the saloon for a few more drinks or even a game of chance.

Then in 1877 the Reverend Ormond W. Wright arrived, the first resident minister in Dodge. At first he preached in the Union Church, but he strongly desired his own Presbyterian Church. Wright proved successful in collecting money because he was more than a preacher; he also was a true Christian who understood the frailties of the flesh, and he was sympathetic to the frontier spirit. For example, in June 1877 his prized horse disappeared, and he was grief-stricken. At this point a deputy sheriff told him that lawmen had apprehended the thief and that the minister had to decide whether the thief should be hanged or shot. The name of this culprit, as reported by the deputy, was Luke McGlue (a name invented by local practical jokers on whom all blame for any of their high jinks was assigned). The Reverend Wright, discovering the prank, laughed good-naturedly, and his horse was returned.[9] His ability to appreciate a joke, even at his own expense, ensured his acceptance, and it caused gamblers and prostitutes, along with

A view of the Union Church after much deterioration. *Courtesy Kansas Historical Society.*

those living north of the tracks, to contribute to his projected Presbyterian church building.

Money in hand, Wright persuaded teamsters to haul lumber to town at minimal cost, and he sought volunteer laborers wherever possible. The hardware, and later the paint, for the building was donated by Zimmerman's hardware store, while a local blacksmith was enlisted to cast bells. The building was located on Central Avenue (previously known as Railroad Avenue). When the building opened in 1880, the Dodge City *Times* noted, "We should have mentioned the matter last week but we thought it best to break the news gently to the outside world. The tender bud of Christianity is only just beginning to sprout, but as 'tall oaks from little acorns grow,' so this infant under the guide and care of

Brother Wright, may grow and spread its foliage like the manly oak of the forest."

Next to erect their own building were the Catholics who, unlike the Protestants of the community, could not attend a nondenominational or Presbyterian service. Father Phillip Colleton, a Jesuit born in Ireland in 1821, had been working as a missionary in Kansas since the 1850s and began celebrating Mass at Fort Dodge in 1869. Three Catholics were among the eight founders of Dodge City: John Riney, operator of the toll bridge, George Kelley, a saloonkeeper, and Dr. T. K. McCarty. Father Colleton added the little community to his string of missions and visited at irregular intervals to administer the sacraments. After his death in 1876, others followed in his footsteps.

The first priest to celebrate Mass in the Union Church building was Father Felix Swembergh, a diocesan priest assigned by his bishop to Wichita and the western missions of Kansas. Bob Wright described Swembergh as "a little fellow with a big heart, with charity for all and malice towards none, no matter what the denomination. He was very highly educated, could speak fluently more than a half dozen different languages." Although the rowdies of Dodge City occasionally played pranks on itinerant preachers, none bothered Father Swembergh—perhaps because he held his services in Dodge's Union Church very early on Sunday mornings before the rough crowd had recovered from Saturday night's fun. Swembergh was joined in western Kansas in August 1875 by Father Boniface Verheyen, who was assigned to the region by the new bishop. They arrived in Dodge shortly thereafter to find it "quiet and practically respectable in the daylight hours."

Bishop Louis M. Fink wanted more in Ford County than a visiting priest, and in 1878 decided to open a monastery—he called it a "Christian Fort"—near Windthorst, a German Catholic community in Ford County. Assigned to this task was Father Ferdinand Wolf, a German-born priest then forty-four years old. Father Ferdinand thereafter roamed the region holding Mass wherever he found Catholics. Visiting Dodge City, he wrote that the city was not as sinful as newspaper reports described, although "things may become worse when more drovers come in, but the Catholic ladies tell me that no one gets hurt who minds his own business." He offered Mass for the first time in Dodge on August 23, 1878, in the school house, and thereafter gathered his flock in the Union Church. Gradually he, like Wright, came to cherish the thought of a church building for the members of his congregation. However, construction did not begin until 1881, by which time the pastor at Windthorst was Father Robert Loehrer. Under his guidance Sacred Heart Catholic Church took shape. The *Globe* reported on July 18, 1882: "The new Catholic Church edifice is beginning to assume tangible proportions and exhibit rare skill in architecture. When wholly completed, it will be one of the strongest and best arranged church buildings on the line of the Santa Fe Railroad." The final cost of the structure was $3500, a sum contributed by cowboys from Texas as well as local citizens. On November 14, 1882, almost 200 people gathered for the service of dedication, conducted by the Very Reverend Anthony Kuhls, who represented Bishop Fink. After the building was placed in service, Father Loehrer worked from there rather than Windthorst, and continued to visit a chain of missions. The first resident priest in Dodge was Father John Begley; his parish included twenty-two counties in southwestern Kansas.[10]

The Methodists had organized a congregation in Dodge in 1874, the first sect to do so, but it was not until 1883 that they had their own building. A Baptist church was organized in 1879 and erected a building in 1885; the Episcopalians, who organized in 1888, completed their building in 1898. Thus during the boom period of Dodge City's history, there were several congregations active in the community, each trying to give the town an image of respectability.

Naturally the school, like the churches, was built on the north side of the railroad tracks. The first school house was built in 1873 on the corner of First Avenue and Walnut Street, a wooden structure erected with voluntary labor, little money, and strong faith

The early Dodge City schoolhouse. *Courtesy Kansas Historical Society.*

in the future. The pioneers of Dodge City, like other frontiersmen of the day, had a firm belief in the value of education, and wanted their children to have every advantage. State law at that time provided for the establishment of county schools, but property taxes were so low that only the rudiments could be provided during the 1870s. After the city was incorporated in 1875, it was eligible to start a city system, and this it did in 1879 when property taxes grew to the point that a new school seemed feasible. In 1879, when the bodies were removed from the old Boot Hill cemetery, construction began on a large, two-story, brick building. This opened in September 1880 and provided—for that day—excellent facilities for elementary and high school students.

Mrs. Margaret A. Walker, a stern-faced disciplinarian, proved equal to the task of teaching the three R's to the first pupils to enroll at Dodge City's school. The first school was crudely built: the desks were uneven, and there were not enough books. Within a year more supplies became available, along with state funds and aid. Keeping pace with this improvement was the increase in the number of students as more families moved to the area. By the 1880s the school was staging theater productions, giving recitations for the parents, and holding musical recitals. Night classes for adults in penmanship and language became available. There were separate teachers for each grade, oratorical contests, and commencement exercises that provided newspaper stories each year.

Parents were concerned not only about the educational and religious training of their children, but also about the medical and dental care available for them as well as for themselves. The buffalo hunter and the cowboy had early resigned themselves to having no medical help on the open range. Inasmuch as most of them were young and strong, their ailments ordinarily were little more than stomach aches and sore throats. For these and similar problems, they dosed themselves with the common patent medicines, such as Universal Liver Remedy, or they applied some herb or poultice cure-all. Others relied on so-called Indian medicine, which was little more than the folklore of the native Americans. An aching tooth was pulled by a blacksmith. For more serious wounds, the cowboy or buffalo hunter relied on self-administered or friend-administered surgery, using kerosene (called coal oil) for a disinfectant and whiskey for an anesthetic. Broken bones were set as common sense and experience dictated, with the result that most people who had suffered such an accident limped or had a twisted arm.

In settlements such as Dodge, however, the local residents wanted something better—although nostrums and patent medicine peddled by itinerant quacks sold extremely well. Most of these had either an alcohol or opium base and did kill pain, although the extravagant claims made for them seldom proved true. These nostrums continued to sell well because medical science was still in its infancy. Most doctors who arrived at a town such as Dodge had not attended a well-known Eastern school. Rather they began as assistants in a drug store, mixing prescriptions until they learned what medicine was prescribed for each ailment, then they served as assistants to a practicing physician until they believed themselves qualified, after which they hung out their shingle and began to practice. There was no state examination, no medical organization, and no inquiries into a high rate of failure. They literally buried their mistakes, hoping to learn something from each.

Dr. Thomas L. McCarty, the pioneer doctor in Dodge who arrived there in 1872, proved a happy exception to the frontier example. After studying medicine at Rush Medical College in Philadelphia, he came west in 1871 at the age of twenty-two to visit a brother-in-law in the Indian Territory. This brought him to Dodge in 1872, where he found conditions to his liking and set up his practice in the drugstore owned by Herman Fringer. Within a short period of time he saw more cuts, broken bones, gunshot and arrow wounds, and victims of accidents with horses than a doctor in the East saw in a lifetime. Fortunately for McCarty, there was a physician stationed at nearby Fort Dodge, Dr. William S. Tremaine, who worked on civilians in his spare time.

Soon other physicians moved to Dodge or received their training there. Dr. W. F. Pine, who later helped found the Ford County Medical Society, began as a clerk in the local drugstore, and Dr. C. A. Milton arrived in town in 1882 to join in practice with McCarty. A fourth doctor, Samuel J. Crumbine, hung out his shingle in Dodge in 1885. Crumbine proved remarkably modern in his thinking, coining the slogans "Swat the Fly" and "Don't Spit on the Sidewalk." Medical science of that day concluded that spitting was the cause of the spread of tuberculosis germs, and Crumbine used his slogan to combat the spread of this dread killer. (Some brick factories imprinted this on their product, which was used to make streets and sidewalks, in order to remind the forgetful not to spit and spread germs.)

Doctors served in other capacities as well as ministering to the sick. McCarty, for example, became the town coroner, while Crumbine became locally well known for his way with sick animals, especially horses. They were also expected to pull teeth, which was the only form of dentistry available. A tooth giving problems was treated with opium or some other pain killer until it no longer would respond to these; then it was pulled.

Dodge did boast one graduate of a dentistry school, although he proved more adept with cards and pistols than with drill and extractors. This was John Henry Holliday, better known as Doc. A native of Georgia, he had practiced his trade until he contracted tuberculosis, after which he moved to Texas hoping for a cure from the dry climate. There he earned his living as a gambler. Several arrests at Fort Griffin, Texas, led to a move to Denver, and then to Dodge City in 1878. By then he was an alcoholic, and Big Nose Kate Elder was soon posing as his wife. In Dodge Doc Holliday settled in room 24 of the Dodge House, drank, gambled, and—occasionally—practiced his craft. An ad in the Dodge City *Times* announced, "J. H. Holliday, Dentist, very respectfully offers his professional services to the citizens of Dodge City and surrounding country during the summer. Office at room No. 24, Dodge House. Where satisfaction is not given, money will be refunded." According to one story, Holliday made the mistake of pulling the wrong tooth from the mouth of Clay Allison, a noted Texas gunfighter, whereupon Allison made Holliday get in the chair and knocked out one of his teeth.[11]

Such stories were chronicled in the local newspapers of Dodge City, all of them weeklies, although by the time the stories appeared most of the residents already knew about the events. Therefore the local newspaperman had to be not only a good reporter but also a humorist or he would have had no readers. The first newspaper in town was the *Messenger*, established by A. W. Moore, formerly a resident of Holton, Kansas, in February 1874. However, business was slow in the months following his arrival, for the trade in buffalo hides was declining and Texas cattle had not yet arrived in large numbers. Moore published his last issue in

"Doc" Holliday. *Courtesy Kansas Historical Society.*

the spring of 1875. A year later, in May 1876, Lloyd and Walter C. Shinn began issuing the *Times*, which proved to be the major paper during the boom period of Dodge City history. In 1878 Lloyd Shinn sold his interest in this paper, for he had become interested in a buffalo tannery in the city. Purchasing his interest was Nicholas B. Klaine, who edited and published the paper until it folded in 1893. A third paper, the Ford County *Globe*, began publication in December 1877; it was edited and published by Daniel M. Frost and W. N. Morphy. In 1878, however, Lloyd Shinn, unsuccessful at his buffalo hide tannery, purchased Morphy's interest and became Frost's partner. The Ford County *Globe* subsequently changed its name several times, appearing under the masthead *Globe Live Stock Journal, Globe-Republican,* Dodge City *Globe,* and, in 1911, the Dodge City *Daily Globe,* the name it retained. The Dodge City *Democrat* began publication in 1884, changing its name later to Dodge City *Journal-Democrat* to match the partisan effort of the *Globe-Republican;* the locale proved healthier for Republicans, and the *Democrat* became the Dodge City *Journal* and then the *High Plains Journal,* a masthead it retained when it became an agricultural publication for a five-state region. One other newspaper tried to find success in Dodge, but failed, the *Kansas Cowboy,* established in 1884 by Samuel S. Prouty.

An example of the type of writing that appealed to local readers appeared in the *Times* on March 24, 1877, involving—as so many stories did—the local nymphs of the prairie:

> The office of City Attorney was thrown into ecstatic convulsions at precisely 4:30 P.M., Monday, by the appearance of Fannie. (Fannie is a beauty, and the color of a Colorado Claro, as found at Beatty & Kelley's.) She complained of one James Cowan (Maduro color) and on the case being tried Mr. [Harry E.] Gryden [city attorney] developed the following facts: That Fanny was peacefully ironing at the residence of Mrs. Curly, when James entered (three-sheets-in-the-wind drunk) called Fanny a soldier b - - - -, throwed her on the floor, elevated her paraphanalia [*sic*], spanked her, and finally busted her a left hander in the right eye, accompanying the same with a kick in the stomache. The City Attorney went to the court and for the defendant, touched up the Louisiana and South Carolina questions, and closed by flinging the star spangled banner over the contraband female, sending the defendant to the regions of the unjust—$5 and costs.

While the saloonkeeper, businessman, and soiled dove went about their business, doctors tried to keep them healthy, and reporters wrote of their frailties, foibles, and successes, there were people in town who tried to bring culture and social uplift to the community. Fraternal organizations quickly made their appearance: the Masons, who had a temple built at a cost of $35,000 by the turn of the century, the Odd Fellows, the Knights of Pythias, the Eagles, Knights and Ladies of Security, and railroad societies, along with a Commercial Club (a forerunner of the modern Chamber of Commerce).[12] Simultaneously there were social and literary clubs for ladies, along with a large bicycle club organized before 1890.

Music also was much appreciated in that day before recordings and radio made it widely available. In 1878 the "good" people of the town conducted a fund-raising drive to secure money to purchase instruments for what was called the "Dodge City Silver Cornet Band." This, said a newspaper account, was done so "Dodge City can toot her own horn." This organization later changed its name to the "Dodge City Brass Band" and then in 1880 to the "Dodge City Cowboy Band." As such it played for parades and other festive occasions; it played when politicians came to town, when new businesses opened, even at funerals. Soon the Cowboy Band began dressing the part, each member wearing broad-brimmed hats decorated with a cattle brand, neckerchiefs, leather chaps, boots, and six-guns. Its fame spread, and soon an enterprising promoter arranged a concert tour for it to Kansas City, Chicago, St. Louis, and elsewhere in the Midwest and East, for people willing to purchase tickets to see "genuine" cowboys performing music with skill and precision. The Cowboy Band was even invited to Washington, D.C., to participate in the inaugural festivities for Benjamin Harrison in March 1889. Chalkley Beeson, co-owner of the Saratoga Saloon and later the Long Branch—and a musician of note—was one of the originators and a driving force in the organization. By 1890, however, the band had become so structured that the members no longer enjoyed it, and it was disbanded.

Another organization highly regarded locally was the Dodge City Fire Company, a volunteer group of young men dedicated to fighting fire, which always was a threat in Western towns built

Dodge City's famed Cowboy Band. *Courtesy Kansas Historical Society.*

mostly of lumber. A prolonged dry spell coupled with warm weather brought great danger, for if one building caught fire the wind would whip it across town and burn everything in its path. The young men of the Fire Company placed empty whiskey barrels at every street corner and along the sidewalks; these were filled with water to be used to extinguish any fire that might begin. Mainly, however, these young men paraded in their uniforms at every opportunity and organized social activities for themselves and their ladies.

This Fire Company involved itself in such activities as organizing the Fourth of July celebration in 1877. This began at two o'clock in the afternoon with a parade involving the Fire Company in uniform, followed by horse racing southwest of town where tents had been erected. The firemen profited by selling ice cream and other refreshments while racehorses vied over a 500-yard course. This was followed by foot and wheelbarrow races, and a ball at the Dodge House with Chalk Beeson's orchestra providing the music. This ended at 2:00 A.M.

The dance was a normal form of entertainment in Dodge. On August 4, 1877, the *Times* reported, "Another of the social hops for which the Dodge House has become famous, was on yesterday evening indulged in by quite a number of our citizens who worship Terpsichore." The *Times* sent a reporter to describe the costumes of the ladies, but, according to the editor, he became intoxicated and gave instead "the following varied description of the paraphernalia of the Lords of Creation":

> Mr. J. F. L. appeared in a gorgeous suit of linsey wolsey, cut bias on the gourd with red cotton handkerchief attachment. . . .
> Mr. H. was modestly attired in a blue larubs wool undershirt, frilled. He is a graceful dancer, but paws too much with his fore legs. His strong point is "the schottish, my dear."
> . . . Mr. J. N.—The appearance of this gentleman caused a flutter among the fair ones; as he trimmed his nails, picked his nose and sailed majestically around the room, the burr of admiration sounded like the distant approach of the No. 3 freight train.

Christmas was another occasion for celebration. For example, on Christmas night, 1878, the Dodge City "Social Club" staged a masquerade ball at the Dodge House. The *Globe* reported on January 1, 1879, that "Champagne and wine flowed freely, but not to excess, and a merrier Christmas night was never enjoyed in Dodge."

Another form of entertainment widely available in Dodge was the theater. However, few women with any pretensions to respectability attended plays except those staged by youngsters in the public school. Several of the saloons on the south side of Front Street, such as the Lady Gay, regularly engaged traveling minstrels and troups to perform, while others, such as the Comique, were designed exclusively for the performing of plays. The productions available in Dodge included *Lady of Lyons, Romeo and Juliet, Rip Van Winkle,* and the ever-popular *Uncle Tom's Cabin,* but most troups performed blackouts and skits of a burlesque nature. In the Comique there was a stage at one end of the house and a bar at the other; near the bar were gambling tables circled by a row of boxes in which the patrons could sit, drink, and view the production. After the show ended, a small band occupied the stage to play for dancing, which continued through the night. For a price hostesses were available to dance with the customers and to lure them to rooms in the back.

One young actor who came to Dodge in July 1878 was Eddie Foy. He arrived with his partner, Jim Thompson, to open at the Comique for a three-month engagement. Coming there from a four-week engagement in Kansas City, they looked out the train window and saw huge piles of buffalo bones. Mistaking these for human bones, Thompson remarked that people in Dodge were dying faster than the undertaker could bury them. Foy's description of Dodge was not flattering: "an ugly but fascinating little town."

The act consisted of blackface and Irish humor. Foy also was joined by one of the female performers, such as Belle Lamont, "the queen of song." Their jokes were hoary with age but considered witty by local patrons. For example, he would say, "Belle, you are my dearest duck," to which she would reply, "Foy, you are trying to stuff me." Between such numbers, another member of the cast, such as Fannie Garrettson, would come out to sing "The Flowers of Kildare," "Killarney," or the maudlin "Home Sweet Home." All this occurred, Foy later recalled, while at the other end of the house there was "the click and clatter of poker chips, balls, cards, dice, wheels and other devices . . . mingled with a medley of crisp phrases—'Thirty-five to one!' 'Get your money down, folks.' 'Eight to one on the colors.' 'Keno!' 'Are you all down, gentlemen?' "

Foy at this time dressed in the loud fashion of the young actor of the day, and he was outspoken in his comments from the stage about Dodge City and cowboys. Several local humorists decided to test the young actor's ability to take as well as give. As he left the theater a few days after he arrived, he was seized, taken to a nearby tree, tied around his neck to the crossbar of a telegraph pole. Given a chance to speak any last words he might have, Foy reportedly stated that he had plenty of words, which could best be spoken at a nearby bar where he stood ready to buy a round of drinks. As a result he was accepted in Dodge, even gaining a reputation for courage. When the Comique closed in September, as the cattle trade ended, Foy and Thompson went on to their next engagement at Leadville, Colorado, but Foy returned the following summer for another long engagement.

Several times Foy came close to the violence associated with the south side of Front Street, but always he avoided it in one way or another. On one occasion he was pressed to join a group of Dodge City citizens going to fight for the Santa Fe Railroad against an army raised by supporters of the Denver and Rio Grande; the squabble was over a pass in Colorado. Bat Masterson approached Foy about joining, whereupon Foy responded that he did not know one end of a pistol from the other. Masterson replied that Foy should carry a sawed-off shotgun which anyone, even an actor, could operate with devastating effect. Foy managed to beg off.

On another occasion, Foy had difficulty with Ben Thompson, who, by all reports, was a cold-blooded killer. Foy did not like Thompson and made little effort to conceal the fact. One evening Thompson came into the Comique and sat down facing Foy. Pulling one of his weapons, Thompson pointed it at Foy's head and said, "Move your head. I aim to shoot that light," indicating a light behind Foy's head. To move would have been cowardly, to stay put would bring death, for Thompson was known to be a man of his word. However, Foy did not move. Instead he stared intently into Thompson's eyes. For some reason Thompson did not shoot. Instead he hesitated. Finally Bat Masterson came over and led Thompson outside. "When they had gone," Foy recalled, "I found my hands shaking so that I couldn't put on my make-up."

Asked why Thompson did not shoot, Foy commented, "A man accustomed to killing tigers would feel himself belittled if he were asked to go on a squirrel hunt."[13]

Dora Hand, an actress, was not as fortunate as Foy. She arrived in Dodge in the summer of 1878 from St. Louis because of her friendship with Fannie Garrettson, the singer. The two had worked together in St. Louis, and after Dora separated from her husband, Theodore Hand, she came to Dodge to join her friend. In Dodge she used her theatrical name Fannie Keenan. That summer she joined Fannie, singing and acting in skits with Foy and Thompson. Next she joined the Hernandez Comedy Company, traveling on to Kinsley and Larned, Kansas. When that company disbanded, she returned to St. Louis, but came back to Dodge in September to have her attorney file for divorce against her husband. While she waited, she was living with Fannie Garrettson in a two-room frame structure located behind the Great Western Hotel. Normally the two women lived in the back room, while Mayor James H. Kelley lived in the front room. However, on the evening of October 3, 1878, Mayor Kelley was ill and went to Fort Dodge to be treated by Dr. W. S. Tremaine. In his absence, Fannie moved into the front room, leaving Dora alone in the back bedroom.

Unknown to either of the two girls, Mayor Kelley had an enemy determined to kill him. James W. Kennedy, son of a Texas cattleman, marketed thousands of cattle in Dodge that summer, had quarreled and fought with Kelley, lost the fight, and departed for Kansas City where he bought a horse. Slipping back into Dodge at night, he came to the window of Kelley's little house and, knowing Kelley slept in the front bedroom, began firing at it through the door. One shot went through the door, ricocheted off the floor, and went under the bed occupied by Fannie Garrettson. Another bullet went through Fannie Garrettson's nightgown, through the wall, and killed Dora Hand. At age thirty-four, "in the full bloom of gayety and womanhood," commented the *Times*, she died. Kennedy was quickly identified as the killer, and a posse set out in pursuit. As he headed south for Texas, he was wounded, captured, and brought back to town to stand trial for murder. However, as the *Globe* noted, "the evidence being insufficient the prisoner was acquitted." Fannie Garrettson decided to move to a safer city.[14]

While the ladies of Dodge City were drinking tea with one another and discussing ways to raise money for a church or a library, men such as Bob Wright were taking positive steps to beautify and uplift their town. Wright, for example, donated the funds to establish Wright Park, which was landscaped in 1883. Meanwhile, the ordinary citizens of the town—men who took a drink regularly and went to the theater, but who neither patronized the brothels nor worried about culture—sought amusement and relaxation in a number of ways. One favorite was hunting, which was done both to provide meat and to entertain. For this purpose many men in town kept hunting dogs. Dodge City dogs, according to Bob Wright, "were known far and wide . . . and justly, too, for they were the best bred of the kind in the world." These were purebred greyhounds, excellent for chasing and killing antelope.

Owner of one of the largest packs of these dogs was Mayor James H. Kelley, nicknamed "Dog Kelley" by most men in town. The morning after the great snowstorm of December 1872, during which a hundred or more buffalo hunters died, Kelley went out to hunt. Half a mile west of town he sighted a herd of antelope and turned his dogs loose. Soon the dogs had caught and killed all the men could carry back to town, so they called off the dogs, loaded their meat, and returned to Dodge. Once back in town Kelley noticed that a favorite dog, "only a pup six months old, but a monster" named Jim, was missing. Therefore he went back to find Jim. A mile past where the hunt had ended, he found a dead antelope; a few miles along he found yet another. Continuing twenty miles west along the Arkansas, he passed several carcasses until at last he came upon Jim, lying tired and exhausted beside yet another dead antelope. The dog had not stopped until it was totally worn out. Kelley brought the animal home on his saddle. Thereafter the men would laugh at the mayor and ask if Jim had quit hunting, to

James "Dog" Kelley, left, and Charles Hungerford. *Courtesy Kansas Historical Society.*

which Kelley would reply, "Not until the antelope does." Kelley was a great dog fancier, often paying as much as $200 for a good animal.[15] In one contest between Kelley and another owner of fine dogs, each turned loose an animal to see which could kill the most antelope. Kelley reportedly won $20,000 when his dog proved superior.[16]

Horses were another animal highly prized at Dodge, and races between favorites occurred frequently. Most of these were quarter-horses—cow ponies valued for their ability to make a quick start and reach maximum speed in a short distance—but there were some thoroughbreds in the vicinity, and all were raced. Bill Tilghman was considered a leading breeder and trainer; one of his animals, a gelding named Chant, won the Kentucky Derby.[17]

Prize fights were another form of entertainment—and cause for betting. The Dodge City *Times* of June 16, 1877, told of one such encounter. The battle was between Nelson Whitman and Red Hanley, also known as "the red bird from the South." The contest had been rumored for several days, but the time and place were kept secret except from the sporting crowd. On a Tuesday morning at 4:30 A.M., after the police had retired for the night, the battle took place in the street in front of the Saratoga saloon. An old gentleman named Colonel Norton acted as referee and time-keeper. According to the account in the *Times*, Whitman was the favorite in the betting, but Hanley fought gamely:

> During the forty-seventh round Red Hanley implored Norton to take Nelson off for a little while till he could have time to put his right eye back where it belonged, set his jaw bone and have the ragged edge trimmed off his ears where they had been chewed the worst. This was against the rules of the ring, so Norton declined, encouraging him to bear it as well as he could and squeal when he got enough. About the sixty-fifth round Red squealed unmistakably and Whitman was declared winner. The only injuries sustained by the loser in the fight were two ears chewed off, one eye busted and the other disabled, right cheek bone caved in, bridge of the nose broken, seven teeth knocked out, one jaw bone

mashed, one side of the tongue chewed off, and several other un-important fractures and bruises. Red retired from the ring in disgust.

Still other forms of fighting could draw a crowd—and produce side bets on the winner. For example, on May 11, 1877, there was a fight called lap-jacket, which also occurred on Front Street, this time in front of the harness shop. A reporter who witnessed the battle wrote:

> We, yesterday, witnessed an exhibition of the African national game of lap-jacket, in front of Shulz' harness shop. The game is played by two colored men, who each toe a mark and whip each other with bull whips. In the contest yesterday, Henry Rogers, called Eph, for short, contended with another darkey for the championship and fifty cents prize money. They took heavy new whips, from the harness shop, and poured in the strokes pretty lively. Blood flowed and dust flew and the crowd cheered until Policeman Joe Mason came along and suspended the cheerful exercise. In Africa, where this pleasant pastime is indulged in to perfection, the contestants strip to the skin, and frequently cut each other's flesh open to the bone.[18]

Perhaps the grandest contest to be staged in Dodge City was the great bullfight of July 4 and 5, 1884. Mayor Alonzo B. Webster generally is credited with originating this idea. By 1884 the end of the boom era was in sight, for the size and number of herds coming north from Texas was diminishing each year, and the prohibition-ists and blue noses were pressing to close saloons and brothels in the city. The thought of staging a Spanish bullfight caught the im-agination of men who did not want to see the free, easy days of the past come to an end. Because their number included many of the town's leading citizens and businessmen, they had little diffi-culty raising $10,000; this they used to purchase a forty-acre tract from A. J. Anthony on the southwest side of town; under the name "Driving Park and Fair Association," they built a bullring with seating for 3500, engaged D. W. "Doc" Barton to supply twelve of the ugliest and meanest bulls in the vicinity, and asked W. K. Moore, a Scotsman practicing law at El Paso del Norte (in Chihuahua, Mexico) to send up five matadors.

Knowing that publicity was necessary if the bullfight was to be a success, the promoters sought all they could get. The reaction was not what they expected. Henry Bergh, Jr., president of the Society for the Prevention of Cruelty to Animals, declared a bullfight contrary to the laws of the United States and said it could not be held. He appealed to Governor George W. Glick of Kansas to stop the fight, but the governor had friends in Dodge City and refused to intervene. Thereupon the S.P.C.A. had the United States district attorney telegraph Mayor Webster that a bullfight was illegal under the laws of the United States. Reportedly Webster replied by wire, "Hell, Dodge City ain't in the United States."

As the great day approached, excitement ran high. The crowds coming into Dodge City were large, assuring the members of the Driving Park and Fair Association a profit. Next came the five matadors from Mexico: Gregorio Gallardo, a tailor; Evarista A. Rivas, superintendent of public works for the state of Chihuahua; Marcus Moyor and Juan Herrera, musicians; and Rodrigo Rivas, an artist. When local citizens invited them to drink, they declined. This deviation from local custom soon caused Dodge residents, along with most Americans, to root for the bulls who, after all, were Americans representing their area's ability to produce ferocious animals.

The twelve bulls selected were given names honoring local citizens and establishments: Ringtailed Snorter, Cowboy Killer, Iron Gall, Loco Jim, Rustler, Sheriff, Lone Star, Ku Klux, Doc, Long Branch, and Opera. Many local citizens went down to watch the cutting out and trying out of these bulls. One man named Brown said shaking a red flag in a bull's face did not make him mad, whereupon someone in the crowd said, "Brown, I will bet you a fifty-dollar suit of clothes you can't shake a red flag in a bull's face without his fighting, and you have the privilege of selecting the most docile bull in this lot of fighters."

Brown promptly accepted. He secured a red shirt, got down into the corral, walked up to the bull he had selected, and waved the shirt in its face. Nothing happened, whereupon Brown turned to walk out of the ring, putting his thumb to his nose and making a victory sign. Just then the bull charged. Somehow it got one horn inserted in Brown's trousers so that he could not escape, and for several minutes the bull butted him into the air. At last he flew free, landing head first in the dirt. "We asked him if his views about bulls had undergone a change," recalled Bob Wright, "but he walked silently along. We wanted to know how he enjoyed the scenery, the last time he went up; but he would not say. He merely went into the cook-house, filled up both barrels of his gun with old nails and screws and scrap iron, and went to interview that bull."[19]

At last came the glorious Fourth of July, and the city was jammed to capacity. The Santa Fe had made a special excursion run to bring hundreds of people who wanted to see the spectacle. Mayor Webster, followed by the Cowboy Band and the matadors in their suits of light, led the procession from town to the bull-ring. Fully a third of the crowd was women and children, but to ensure that no good women had to sit with bad ones the dance hall ladies of Dodge were directed to one special portion of the seats. Naturally the more boisterous and drunken cowboys also were directed to that area; there they drank, hugged the girls, hooted with laughter, and enjoyed themselves in unrestrained fashion, while across the way the good people watched in silence as the bullfight proceeded. The temperature had passed the 100-degree mark by the time the first bull was turned into the ring.

However, the plains bulls showed little enthusiasm for their part in the spectacle. Several had to be led from the ring in disgrace, for they refused to charge despite the pics inserted in their shoulders and the waving of the red cape. When the chief matador, Gallardo, finally got one bull to charge in the traditional manner and then killed it with his sword, there were some cheers from the crowd. A few days later the Ford County *Globe* reported,

The arena constructed for the bullfight. *Courtesy Kansas Historical Society.*

"Thus ended the first day's bull fight in Dodge City, and for all we know the first fight on American soil. The second day's fighting, with the exception of the killing of the last animal in the ring, was more interesting than the first."[20] There were no more bull fights in Dodge; one was enough for American taste.

During most of the year, entertainment was not organized. Each man provided his own or enjoyed another man's amusement by listening to the gossip about it. Frequently in the town the talk was of the latest practical joke. Largely forgotten in this age of commercial entertainment has been the 19th-century penchant for the practical joke. On the frontier the sudden, unexpected prank—if one was not the butt of the joke—was a fine art form. Sometimes these jokes were old standards, never losing their humor by repetition; at other times the practical joke was something new, something planned in exquisite detail and carried out at some expense and/or risk. A good practical joke caught the public imagination and became a topic of conversation for days, relieving the monotony and boredom of life. Generally the butt of the practical joke was the person who made himself vulnerable through ignorance—*i.e.*, the greenhorn or traveling man—or through overindulgence in strong liquor. The reaction of the person on whom a joke had been played was also important; to get angry was to brand oneself a target for further humor, while the ability to laugh at one's predicament brought welcome and camaraderie.

A favorite trick of the crowd in Dodge City addicted to practical joking, usually called the "gang," was the Indian scare. A newcomer who indicated a desire to fight Indians or who bragged about his courage in past encounters with Indians was the usual victim. For example, in April 1877 Elias Kahn, came to town representing Kahn and Company, a clothing firm in Kansas City, and bragged that in past encounters with Indians he had acted with great bravery. Very quickly he was invited to go hunting by Mayor Kelley and two friends, while another seven participants dressed in Indian clothing, painted their faces, and rode out in a roundabout way to intercept the hunters. When Kelley led Kahn out of town to hunt, word spread of the impending "Indian attack," and local residents hurried to rooftops or to Boot Hill to get a view of the battle. A few miles out of Dodge the mayor told Kahn to keep a sharp lookout because the most vicious Indians on the plains had been seen in the vicinity. About four miles out of town, Kahn and the mayor suddenly saw the "Indians" riding at them full tilt, yelling in a blood-curdling manner. Kahn, who had been supplied with a revolver loaded with blanks, turned his horse around and rode toward Dodge at full speed. Seeing all the people on house and hilltop, he thought at first the town also was under siege, but, learning the truth, he joined with another crowd of practical jokers and pelted the "Indians" with rotten eggs as they returned from their attack.

On one occasion, however, the Indian attack miscarried. This occurred when P. L. Beatty rode out with a newcomer and was greeted by yells and the firing of weapons (containing blanks). At first the stranger turned and ran in satisfactory fashion, but suddenly he found his courage, reached into his saddlebag and pulled out a weapon loaded with real bullets, and fired at his pursuers. Suddenly it was the Indians who lost their courage and rode fast to get away. When they returned to town, they were greeted by shouts of laughter and derision.[21]

Another favorite trick on the greenhorn was to invite him to participate in a snipe hunt. The snipe, he was told, was a bird that made delicious eating. The victim would be led to a swampy area along the banks of the Arkansas and told to wait there with a sack held open with a lantern at the mouth; the snipe would be attracted by the light and would run inside the sack. When it was full, he was to close it and trap the birds inside. The oldtimers then said they would go out and drive snipes into the trap. Naturally they went home to get a warm night's sleep, leaving the greenhorn snipe hunter down at the swamp. Sooner or later even the greenest of them understood the joke and came wandering back to town.[22]

Another favorite trick of the gang was the use of hokey-pokey (bisulphite of carbon) which, when applied to the skin of an animal, drove the poor beast almost wild. A cowboy riding into Dodge and showing great pride in his horsemanship was a sure target for this trick. "Never yet did I see a man who could retain his seat on a doped horse," wrote Bob Wright of this trick. On one occasion a stranger came to town on an excellent piece of horseflesh just as an auction was in progress. "Mr. Auctioneer," the rider announced, "I am going east and have no use for this horse, or I would not part with him. He is all that he appears to be, has all the gaits of a saddler, is sound as a dollar, and gentle as a dog. He never ran away, will stand without hitching, and was never known to buck, plunge, or kick." Naturally one of the gang soon doped the animal, whereupon he reared, bucked, ran, and plunged until he dislodged his rider. After the animal became quiet, the stranger caught him, mounted, and then turned to the crowd to state, "Gentlemen, I beg your pardon. I lied to you, but upon my word I never saw this horse act badly before, in any way. I withdraw him from the market."[23]

Another use for hokey-pokey, resulting in great fun for the town and little for the victim, occurred when a band of Gypsies arrived at Dodge, bringing with them a bear, several chimpanzees, some horses, and twenty to thirty dogs. On the first day the Gypsies tried to stage a horse race, but all their horses went crazy when hokey-pokey was applied to them. The next day the Gypsy women came to town with chimpanzees to perform tricks and earn coins; when the chimps were doped, they went for the men who applied it, causing howls of merriment from the crowd and a frantic effort by the Gypsy women to control the chimps. The third day the Gypsies announced their special performance: the bear would be tied on a rope several hundred feet long and then given a bone; then the pack of twenty to thirty dogs would be turned loose. Because both bear and dogs were hungry, all were anxious to have the bone and would fight for it. This time the program did not go as planned, however, for just as the bear was turned loose he was given an extremely large dose of hokey-pokey, as were the nearby dogs, chimpanzees, and other animals belonging to the Gypsies. "The results were highly satisfactory," wrote Bob Wright. Every animal went crazy, the bear running to the end of his rope and dragging his Gypsy captors along until he turned and ran at them, swatting dogs out of his way as he proceeded. "The bear had the right of way and used it," Wright noted of this performance. The town marshall at that time, Low Warren, tried to preserve order and keep people out of the way of the bear, but despite his great size he was bowled over in the melee. "The howling, screaming, moaning, and acrobatic performances of people and animals were certainly worth the price of admission," Wright recalled. "When the Gypsies could come to a realization of what had happened, the women made a charge on the gang, armed with sticks, stones, and everything that would serve as a weapon of offensive warfare. The disregard for polite language was very noticeable, and the confusion of tongues was bewildering."[24]

The drunk was often the butt of a joke. One escapade involved a bear, this one the property of James H. Kelley, the saloonkeeper who had served as mayor. He had acquired the animal as a cub and raised it. Known as Paddy-the-bear, she spent most of her days chained in Kelley's back yard, where pranksters loved to slip her drinks of whiskey. Paddy came to love the whiskey but to hate the pranks played on her, and she learned to hide whenever possible. One night she met with a traveling salesman well known in Dodge as a hard worker and equally hard drinker. On this occasion the salesman had gone on a monumental drunk, ending in his ground-floor room in the Dodge House where he drifted off to sleep thinking he was seeing snakes. Paddy, meanwhile, had broken her chain and was seeking a place to hide when she spied the open window of the salesman's room. Climbing in, the bear slipped under the salesman's bed; it was so tight a fit that when the animal breathed the bed rose and fell. Just at breakfast time the salesman awoke to find his bed unsteady and concluded that he had a bad case of delirium tremens. In great fright the salesman reached out to the night table beside his bed, grabbed a water tumbler, and threw it under the bed, striking Paddy who reared in fright, lifting bed and salesman with him. The salesman tipped to one side, throwing his hands to the floor to break his fall. This brought his head down under the level of the bed, and he found himself looking directly into the black eyes of the bear. Fearing that he indeed had a bad case of delirium tremens, the salesman rushed screaming out of his room into the dining room of the Dodge House, still in his night clothes. There, in a room crowded with guests and waitresses, he knocked over one of the girls bearing a tray loaded with dishes. All the salesman could say was, "Boys, I've got 'em! By God, I've got 'em!"[25]

Paddy at last was teased to the point where she became a public menace and had to be killed. Kelley had the job done by a local butcher who put Paddy's carcass on sale as meat in December 1883. A reporter for the *Democrat* noted her passing:

> The boys who in days of yore petted and fondled her, now stand silently gazing on her well rounded buttox, licking their chops in anticipation of bear steak at twenty-five cents per pound, and

envying the fellow to whom she, by will no doubt, left her over-coat. In life she was a prominent member of the gang, in death she held her own. She weighed more than the city Mayor, was a better solo bass singer than the Police Judge, was as moral as the biblical Joseph and sold for more money, and could drink more whisky than her biographer. Requiescat in pace.

Another prank on a drunk involved a drunken lawyer who passed out in the Alhambra saloon one day. Friends put him in a funeral shroud, dusted his face with talcum to give it the pallor of the dead, and put him in a coffin. This was surrounded with a wreath of sunflowers, while candles were lit at his head and feet. When he awakened, it was to find mourners gathered around his coffin reading his epitaph, "Gone, but we don't know where." He jumped from the coffin, staggered into the saloon, saw his reflection in the mirror, and swore off the demon rum.

On another occasion, when an organ grinder arrived in town with a dancing bear, the gang found a sleeping drunk, poured honey over him, and turned the bear loose. The drunk awoke to find the bear contentedly licking away at him. Screaming in fear, the drunk jumped up and ran through town, the bear in pursuit, followed by the organ grinder fearful of losing his animal.[26]

The practical jokes were endless. A cigar salesman would be told that Luke McGlue would pay for his entire stock of cigars. These would then be distributed around town. When the salesman went looking for the fictitious McGlue, he would find almost every man in town smoking, saying McGlue had given them the cigar. Or an outhouse would be moved three feet back so that the sleepy house owner stumbling out to heed the call of nature would fall into the pit. A town Romeo would suddenly be bombarded with love letters from fictitious females proposing marriage, followed by the appearance of a fat, ugly (hired) Indian squaw showing up in town swearing that the lover boy had promised to marry her. The gang would side with her, grab the unfortunate Romeo, drag the couple to the town plaza, and a bogus traveling minister would perform the ceremony; afterward the groom, half out of his mind with worry, would be told of the prank. Some of these jokes were spur-of-the-moment affairs; others were elaborately planned and carried through. But all provided merriment, were told and re-told with relish, and often brought about a change in behavior.

No one was immune from such pranks, not the doctor, sheriff, or judge. The *Times* reported on September 29, 1877, one such case:

> Judge R. W. Evans held court last Saturday. The case was one of great interest, and about two hundred people were present. It was Mr. Brown of Garfield vs. somebody—Mr. Brown could not find out exactly who. But these are the particulars: While Mr. Brown was inoffensively taking a drink at Beatty & Kelley's some one in-geniously set fire to the lower extremities of his coat from behind. Mr. Brown exhibited great presence of mind by shedding his coat as soon as he felt the flames. Suit was brought to find out the guilty party and punish him. Owing to the great crowd the case was tried in Mayor Kelly's hall. But no decision was reached, ow-ing to the fact that eggs were too freely used to suit his Honor, the Judge. The Judge took his seat with his usual gravity, and was beginning to investigate the case, when an egg struck him some-where near the back of the head, and as eggs usually do when they strike, it scattered considerably. The Judge immediately adjourned court and proceeded to hunt soap and water. Mr. Brown says he has no faith in Dodge City courts, and will appeal his case to the Governor.

Especially vulnerable were those seeking to bring culture to Dodge, such as Dr. J. Graves Brown who arrived in the city to give a lecture on the occult sciences. Engaging the Lady Gay saloon as an auditorium, he had just begun to speak when someone yelled, "You lie!" To this he responded by giving his learned background on the subject of his talk. This brought the response, "That's an-other damn lie!" Bat Masterson, who had been hired to protect the lecturer, jumped to his feet and yelled, "Stand up, you measly skunk, so I can see you." Half a dozen men arose and gunfire broke out—hitting only the lights. The audience, knowing that most of the shots were blanks, nevertheless yelled and ducked outside. The lecture was over. Dr. Brown soon left town seeking a more refined place to speak.[27]

Dodge City by the late 1870s had a city hall, a church, and a jail, but it was no quiet, civilized village. These were exuberant young men filled with the fun of living. Most often their pranks ended in general merriment and laughter, but on occasion tempers flared, guns were drawn, and the smell of gunpowder filled the air. Then the town's peace officers were called to restore order, although many of those wearing badges little understood—or believed in—the laws they swore to uphold when they took their oaths of office.

A Wicked Little Town

By the late 1870s Dodge City had a reputation for evil and wickedness. Visiting newspapermen constantly referred only to the worst aspects of its citizens and visitors, painting a picture of unrestrained licentiousness. A letter in the Washington, D.C., *Evening Star* of January 1, 1878, stated, "Dodge City is a wicked little town. Indeed, its character is so clearly and egregiously bad that one might conclude, were the evidence in these later times positive of its possibility, that it was marked for special Providential punishment." The editor of the Hays City *Sentinel* wrote after a visit, "Dodge is the Deadwood of Kansas. Her incorporate limits are the rendezvous of all the unemployed scallawagism in seven states. Her principal business is polygamy without the sanction of religion, her code of morals is the honor of thieves, and decency she knows not."[1] A tourist in Dodge wrote the *Times* a letter in 1877 stating, "Dodge has many characteristics which prevent its being classed as a town of strictly moral ideas and principles, notwithstanding its being supplied with a church, a court-house, and a jail. . . . Fast men and fast women are around by the score, seeking whom they may devour, hunting for a soft snap, taking him in for cash, and many is the Texas cowboy who can testify as to their ability to follow up successfully the callings they have embraced in quest of money."[2]

Front Street in the 1880s. Note the sign prohibiting the carrying of firearms. *Courtesy Kansas Historical Society.*

The editors of newspapers in other cities in Kansas, some of them in competition with Dodge for the cattle trade, painted a black picture of the town whenever possible. The Yates Center *News* stated, "Dodge City. A Den of Thieves and Cut Throats— The Whole Town in League to Rob the Unwary Stranger." The Hays *Sentinel* asserted, "The town is full of prostitutes and every house is a brothel"; and the North Topeka *Times* declared that Dodge was "a perfect paradise for gamblers, cut throats and 'girls.' "[3]

Because of this reputation, some travelers feared for their lives as they approached the town. For example, one young man named Herbert wrote his father on May 7, 1877, when he was still fifteen miles from Dodge, "Have laid over here to wait for a larger crowd so as to be perfectly safe going through Dodge."[4] To this letter, published in the *Times*, the editor added, "The card was evidently written while awaiting reinforcements to assist in making a charge through our city, but not mailed until they had run the gauntlet and halted to take a breath at a safe distance on the west side." Generally this young man's view of Dodge City was the one prevailing in many parts of the United States and was well expressed in an anecdote widely circulated at the time. According to this story a drunken cowboy got on the train about thirty miles from Dodge. When the conductor asked his destination in order to compute his fare, the cowboy drunkenly stated, "I want to go to hell!" To this the conductor replied, "All right; give me a dollar and get off at Dodge."[5]

Many of the businessmen in Dodge realized that such a hard reputation was to their advantage, for the cattlemen and cowboys coming up the trail from Texas, along with the buffalo hunters, wanted a wide-open city in which to spend their money for what they considered fun. During its earliest years the city was able to give its visitors exactly what they wanted, for there was no law in town. Although Ford County had been created by the state legislature in 1867, it was not organized until 1873, and thus had no sheriff until the special election on June 5 that year. Nor was the town itself incorporated as a third-class city until November 1875; therefore it had no town marshal or policemen until that time. With no law officers, no courts, and no jail, each person was responsible for his own safety and the protection of his property.

The first recorded killing in Dodge occurred in September 1872. A black man named Black Jack was shot, for no apparent reason, by a gambler known only as Denver, in front of Beatty & Kelley's saloon during some excitement when a crowd had gathered and several shots were fired. No one noticed who had killed the black at the time, although the gambler bragged of the incident years later.[6] Almost immediately after, Jack Reynolds, a rough man shot six times by a track layer working for the Santa Fe Railroad, was killed. Then in November J. M. Essington, owner of the Essington Hotel, was shot by his cook; afterward the name of the hotel was changed to Dodge House. George M. Hoover, a pioneer resident, recalled in 1903 that during the first year of the town's existence there were at least fifteen men killed in Dodge City.[7]

Some place had to be selected for burying these bodies. The site chosen was a desolate hill to the west of town and half a mile north of the Arkansas. Little vegetation other than some clumps of buffalo grass covered this useless hill; rocks protruded from the ground in places, while white gypsum deposits could be seen on it in other places. Because it was high and had good drainage—and was suitable for no other purpose—it seemed a natural place to bury the dead. When a cowboy, gambler, buffalo hunter, or transient died, he was placed in a hastily constructed pine box, carried by wagon to the edge of town, and buried in a grave. Sometimes a wooden cross or headboard was erected bearing the name of the deceased—if known—but the writing soon faded and the identity of the person buried there was forgotten. Such was the final resting place of the person without friends, money, home, and, on occasion, name. Because so many of these people died, according to the Western expression, "with their boots on," this cemetery was called Boot Hill.

Eventually there were approximately thirty mounds of earth on Boot Hill, including the remains of one woman, Alice Chambers. By 1878, however, this piece of real estate had become too valuable to be used as a cemetery, and the Town Company, which owned the property, sold it to Herman Fringer and Samuel Marshall, who intended to subdivide it into lots for homes (part of it also became the site of the new school house). Meanwhile, the more proper residents of Dodge City used the cemetery at Fort Dodge to inter their dead. With the closing of Boot Hill, the town needed a permanent cemetery. Robert M. Wright, James H. Kelley, P. L. Beatty, Samuel Marshall, and Dr. William S. Tremaine thereupon advanced the capital needed to purchase a plot of land from the Town Company; located about half a mile northeast of town, this was called Prairie Grove Cemetery. The company sold lots for $5 each or $25 for a family plot. John W. Straughn, the county coroner, jailer, and deputy sheriff, moved the bodies from Boot Hill to this new resting place in January 1879. When the task was completed near the end of January 1879, Boot Hill was no more.[8]

By late 1872 several merchants were so concerned about the wild state of affairs in the city and the threat to their property this posed that they pooled their resources to hire their own marshal. The person occupying this position had no legal authority for wearing a badge and enforcing a rough kind of justice, but public opinion sanctioned his actions. By February 1873, however, the lawlessness was such that the businessmen formed a vigilance committee and began dispensing hemp justice in rude fashion. That month members of the committee killed two men in a dance hall and ordered five others to leave town. In March the committee killed a buffalo hunter named McGill, who had been shooting indiscriminately in town. When the vigilance committee proved effective, many members of the gambling fraternity decided to join it, and by June that year they outnumbered the merchants and could act with impunity. On June 3 some drunken members of the committee, part of the wild crowd, attacked William Taylor, a black servant in the employ of Colonel Richard I. Dodge, shot one of the mules leading his wagon, and then fatally wounded him. Colonel Dodge was so outraged that he wired the governor of the state for permission to arrest the perpetrators; with this permission in hand, he sent troops to town who arrested Bill Hicks, who later was convicted for his part in the affair.

At last Ford County was organized and an election for the office of sheriff was held. The result was the loose formation of two political factions in Dodge City, a split intensified by elections for mayor and city council after the town was incorporated in 1875. On one side were arrayed those people who wanted to keep the saloons and houses of prostitution open and to allow gambling to flourish; on the other side were those who wanted to shut down saloons and brothels and conform to the general level of morality

Colonel Richard Irving Dodge. *Courtesy Kansas Historical Society.*

153

in the United States at that time. For the first several years the exponents of a wide-open town, known as the "Dodge City gang," controlled the city and county and set the tone in it. Thus they could ignore the prohibition laws passed by the state legislature of Kansas, leaving their town one of the few that were wet in the state; similarly they could evade or disregard statutes forbidding prostitution and gambling. The gamblers and saloonkeepers naturally sided with those merchants who wanted few restrictions on life in the city, and from their ranks came many of the early peace officers. This enraged the moralists of the city, who wanted all state laws enforced, and fought bitterly at election time to win the offices of sheriff, mayor, and city councilman. The newspapers joined in this factionalism, the *Times* generally siding with the Dodge City gang and the *Globe* with the moralists.

Elected sheriff in 1873 was Charles E. Bassett, also known as "Senator." Inasmuch as he also had to serve as an officer of the court for several of the unorganized counties to the south and west, he proved a popular officer with the gang. Apparently he confined his activities to pursuing an occasional horse thief or train robber, allowing events to take their course in Dodge City itself. Only after the cattle—and cattlemen—began arriving in large numbers did the attitude of law enforcement officials become important. Under the laws of the state of Kansas, a sheriff could succeed himself only once, and thus in the fall of 1877 Bassett was not a candidate for reelection. On January 14, 1878, he was out of office and became under-sheriff to his replacement and then city marshal in April that year.[9]

When Dodge was incorporated on November 2, 1875, a special election followed on December 1 that year. P. L. Beatty, part owner of a saloon, became the first mayor, serving until the following April when, at the regular election, George M. Hoover was elected chief executive officer of the town. He, in turn, was succeeded in April 1877 by James H. Kelley, who held the office until 1881. All three men were saloonkeepers and liquor dealers and thus members of the Dodge City gang.

Appointed city marshal by Mayor Beatty was Lawrence E. "Larry" Deger, a huge man of almost 300 pounds who formerly had been a freighter. At first Deger sympathized with the gang. By 1877, when Kelley was elected mayor, many people in Dodge thought there would be a change in the marshal's office. However, Kelley reappointed Deger, who then took on two assistants: Joseph W. Mason, known locally as the "Apollo of Dodge" because of his dandified dress, his good looks, and his winning way with the ladies; and Edward J. Masterson, oldest brother of a remarkable family that supplied Dodge City with three lawmen. The salary for all three was $75 a month.

Ed Masterson was twenty-five-years old when he was appointed an assistant marshal on June 5, 1877. Born in Illinois, he had come to Kansas with his parents, brothers, and sisters in the early 1870s to settle about fourteen miles northeast of Wichita. There he and two younger brothers, William Barclay (or Bartholomew) "Bat" Masterson, born in 1853, and James P. Masterson, born in 1855, grew to manhood. All were involved by 1872 in hunting buffalo, enduring the cold, loneliness, and danger to secure the valuable hides. For a time Ed worked in James Kelley's establishment, leaving to hunt buffalo from time to time. Then in 1877 he was appointed assistant marshal, at which time one of the newspapers stated, "He is not very large, but there are not many men who would be anxious to tackle him a second time. He makes a good officer."[10]

His brother Bat, who eventually became the best known of the brothers, continued to hunt buffalo in 1874, participating in the famed battle of Adobe Walls in the Texas Panhandle. By 1875 Bat was back in Dodge City in time to be listed in the census taken that year as a teamster. During the next two years he apparently moved about the West, reportedly receiving a wound in Sweetwater, Texas, in a gunfight with an Army sergeant; the wound caused him to walk with the aid of a cane for some time. Back in Dodge City early in June 1877, he intervened in a police affair when Marshal Deger, after arresting gambler Bobby Gill

Bat Masterson. *Courtesy Kansas Historical Society.*

(Robert Gilmore), was kicking him along toward the jail. Masterson stopped the kicking by wrapping his arm around Deger's neck, thereby allowing Gill to escape; then policeman Joe Mason helped arrest Masterson and beat Bat over the head with a pistol. Judge D. M. Frost fined Masterson $25 for his part in the affray, while Gill, later arrested by Ed Masterson, was fined only five dollars. Part of Masterson's fine was remitted by Mayor Kelley, and shortly thereafter Bat was chosen under-sheriff by Charles Bassett.[11]

The third brother, James, likewise settled in Dodge. There he became co-owner, with Ben Springer, of the Lady Gay dance hall and saloon. He was appointed to the Dodge City police force on June 1, 1878.[12]

Joining this trio as a law officer, gambler, and member of the Dodge City gang was Wyatt Berry Stapp Earp. Born in Monmouth, Illinois, on March 19, 1848, he moved with his family to Iowa shortly thereafter. His older brothers served during the Civil War, while young Wyatt and the remainder of the family moved to San Bernardino, California, in 1864. Wyatt left there in 1869 to make his way to Lamar, Missouri, where a brother, Newton Earp, lived; there he ran unsuccessfully against his brother for the position of town marshal. Then on January 10, 1870, he married. His wife died a few months later and Wyatt, after quarreling with her family, drifted into Kansas. There followed a stint of buffalo hunting before he moved through Wichita, Kansas, during its boom period as a cattle town. During these years Earp became a cardsharp, a man with a narrow face and drooping mustache who dressed in fancy white shirts. He served briefly as a city policeman in Wichita—from April 21, 1875, to April 19, 1876, but on April 5, 1876, he was arrested and fined for violating the peace. Two weeks later he was fired. A month later the city commission went on record recommending that the vagrancy laws be enforced against him and his brother Jim, who had been driving a hack in the city. In Dodge he was hired as assistant marshal by Larry Deger, and served from May to September 1876. Afterward he apparently went to Deadwood, South Dakota, returning to Dodge in July

Wyatt Earp. *Courtesy National Archives.*

1877 and quarreling with Frankie Bell, a drunken prostitute. For this he was fined one dollar.[13] The following summer Earp again was in Dodge, and in July was appointed an assistant marshal.[14] He and the Mastersons were deeply involved in the affairs of Dodge for the next several years.

During the season for shipping cattle in 1877 there were the usual problems of keeping order in Dodge: fistfights, gunfights, quarreling prostitutes, horse thefts, and even a few jailbreaks. And there was a major confrontation with the soldiers of Fort Dodge. The troopers, when they came to town, were frequently the butt of jokes and of unprovoked verbal and physical attacks. Moreover, the town's gamblers flagrantly cheated the soldiers out of their pay. In June Colonel William H. Lewis grew angry at the mistreatment of his men and, gathering a force of men, marched into town with weapons. According to a report of the incident in the paper, "a pale gray look" appeared on the faces of several of the gambling and rough crowd and "their chins quivered." Just as the angry soldiers seemed about to exact justice, a respected member of the local community came out under a flag of truce, arbitrated the dispute satisfactorily, and took the colonel to the Dodge House for drinks.

A year later a confrontation between soldiers and the gamblers was not settled so easily. Early in August 1878 a group of soldiers, fleeced of their money in one of Dodge's saloons, became angry and vocal, whereupon they were thrown into the street by force. When they returned to the fort to complain to their company commander, the officer carefully made preparations for a reprisal. After waiting a day and night, during which time the gamblers were prepared for trouble, the officer marched his company into town in formation, dispersed them into position, and fired several volleys through the side of the saloon. In order to avoid casualties, he deliberately had them aim too high to hit the patrons inside. The result was a renewed respect for the soldiers at the nearby fort.[15]

Late in 1877 one major change in Dodge City's peace officers was effected. Marshal Larry Deger increasingly was at odds with Mayor James Kelley. The quarrel grew more open in July that year when Deger arrested Charles Ronan, the bartender at Kelley's saloon, and deposited him in the city jail, which constituted the ground floor of a two-story wooden building just south of the railroad tracks on Front Street (the second floor of this structure housed city offices and the police court). The mayor, learning of this arrest, angrily ordered Deger to release Ronan. When Deger refused, Kelley suspended him from office and ordered Ed Masterson and Joe Mason to arrest the marshal. That afternoon the city council reversed Kelley's order, reinstated the marshal, and smoothed over the affair.

By late fall the quarrel between the two men had grown, however, and it came to a head over the election of a new sheriff that November. By state law Charles Bassett could not be a candidate for reelection, and the mayor, along with other members of the Dodge City gang, chose to support Bat Masterson for the job. Their newspaper, the *Times*, on October 13 commented, " 'Bat' is well known as a young man of nerve and coolness in cases of danger. He has served on the police force of this city and also as under-sheriff, and knows just how to gather in the sinners. He is qualified to fill the office and if elected will never shrink from danger." His opponents in the race were George F. Hinkle and Larry Deger. On election day, November 6, Bat received three votes more than Deger and thus won the office—just one day after his brother Ed was wounded in a shootout at the Lone Star dance hall and saloon by a cowboy, Bob Shaw, who was outraged at being cheated out of his money by a gambler.[16]

This election out of the way, Mayor Kelley removed Deger as town marshal, appointing Ed Masterson in his place. Sheriff Bassett then resigned, allowing Bat Masterson to take his place as temporary sheriff until the beginning of his regular term in January 1878. Bassett then became under-sheriff as well as assistant town marshal. The gang thereby had total control of law enforcement in Dodge, and, according to the *Times*, the situation met "with the approbation of our people."[17] Apparently it did, for on April 2, 1878, the entire slate of candidates for local office put forward by the gang was elected: James Kelley as mayor, along with Chalk Beeson, Walter Straeter, John Newton, D. D. Colley, and James Anderson as councilmen. Dodge City was wide open that year when the Texas cattle came north. Yet there was a price to pay for having such a town—as Ed Masterson learned on April 9.

About 10:00 P.M. that evening pistol shots rang out at one of the saloons on the south side of the railroad tracks where no attempt was made to disarm anyone (north of the tracks the carrying of weapons was prohibited). Marshal Ed Masterson and one of his policemen, Nat L. Haywood, arrived on the scene to find six cowboys just off the trail drunk and firing their pistols. Masterson disarmed one of the cowboys, Jack Wagner, the drunkest and most outspoken, after which the music and dancing were renewed. Just as Masterson and Haywood stepped out of the building onto the sidewalk, Wagner came out with another pistol, whereupon Masterson moved to disarm him again and a scuffle ensued. Haywood tried to help Masterson, but A. M. Walker, Wagner's boss, drew his pistol, pointed it at Haywood, and told him to stay out of the affair. When Haywood persisted in his attempt to help, Walker stuck his pistol in the policeman's face and pulled the trigger. The pistol misfired, but Haywood was so frightened that he ran up the street to get help. At this point Wagner managed to get his pistol out, and he shot Marshal Ed Masterson in the abdomen at close range, causing his clothing to catch fire.

Sheriff Bat Masterson also had heard the shooting and was moving toward the scene when, some forty feet away, he saw the shooting. After Ed was wounded, other shots followed in rapid succession. The newspaper account said that shots from Ed's revolver hit Wagner in the belly and Walker was hit in the lung and the right arm. Ed Masterson then staggered across the street into Hoover's saloon and died about an hour later. Wagner lived about twenty hours and then was buried in Boot Hill. Walker somehow recovered enough to travel with his father to Kansas

City and then return to Texas. Ed Masterson, after a large funeral service conducted by Reverend O. W. Wright, was taken to Fort Dodge for burial,[18] for as yet Dodge City had no cemetery for its decent citizens. After Ed's death, former sheriff Charles Bassett was appointed city marshal, and no change was made in the gang's policy of allowing the fun to continue south of the railroad tracks.

Nor was that policy changed in July when another peace officer was killed. Harry T. McCarty, a surveyor and painter, had been appointed a deputy United States Marshal about the time of Ed Masterson's death, but had little to do other than transport an occasional prisoner or serve a warrant. On July 13 he was at the Long Branch saloon when a chuckwagon cook, described by the newspaper as a "half-witted . . . and quarrelsome wretch," departed from the saloon to return to his camp and then turned around and came back to town. McCarty was standing at the bar in conversation with the bartender when the cook, known as Thomas "Limping Tom" O'Hara (or O'Haran, alias Tom Roach), re-entered the saloon, slipped behind McCarty, and snatched McCarty's pistol. When McCarty turned around, O'Hara shot him. He died an hour later, and was buried in Pleasant Grove Cemetery—which he had surveyed three months earlier.[19]

Almost two weeks later—on July 26—the music of the six-shooter again was heard in the early morning hours in Dodge. According to the account in the *Times*, "three or four herders were paying their respects to the city and its institutions, and as is usually their custom, remained until about 3 o'clock in the morning, when they prepared to return to their camp." They buckled on their revolvers, which they were not allowed to wear around town, mounted their horses, and began shooting their pistols. One of the bullets entered a nearby saloon, but hit no one. Policemen Wyatt Earp and Jim Masterson arrived on the scene and exchanged volleys with the drunken cowboys, whereupon the cowboys headed for the bridge south of town to cross the Arkansas. Earp and Masterson followed to arrest them. A few yards across the bridge one of the cowboys, George Hoy, was so weakened by a wound one of the policemen had inflicted that he fell from his horse. When Earp and Masterson stopped to see about him, the others made their escape. Hoy died on August 21 and was buried in Pleasant Grove Cemetery.[20]

During these months Bat Masterson was proving himself a good sheriff everywhere except in the saloons south of the tracks. He pursued horse thieves and train robbers with dispatch, and he transported prisoners sentenced to a term in jail to the penitentiary. Eddie Foy, who came to town that summer to play at the Comique, described Masterson as "a trim good-looking young man with a pleasant face and a carefully barbered mustache, well-tailored clothes, hat with a rakish tilt and two big silver-mounted, ivory-handled pistols in a heavy belt."[21]

Despite his work, and that of the town marshal and his policemen, at least six shooting scrapes occurred in Dodge during one week in September. Then in October came the murder of Dora Hand, while assaults and lesser shootings were common through October and November. By December the jail contained O'Hara, the killer of U.S. Deputy Marshal McCarty; James Kennedy, who had shot Dora Hand; Henry Gould, arrested for assault with intent to kill; Dan Woodward, held on the same charge as Gould; and two other men under arrest for lesser offenses. That month two additional prisoners arrived, horse thieves brought in from Fort Elliott, Texas. Four of these prisoners escaped during the second week in December by sawing through their bars; subsequently three of them were recaptured. In retrospect the year 1878 was exciting indeed, containing the murder of two peace officers, various shootings, a jail break, even an Indian scare when Chief Dull Knife and a band of Cheyenne Indians fled their reservation in the Indian Territory and moved across western Kansas. The gang controlling Dodge did attempt to make the gamblers, saloon-keepers, and prostitutes pay most of the cost of keeping the peace that year, for in August the city council passed an ordinance against gambling and prostitution within the city limits. Thereafter police officers regularly arrested gamblers and prostitutes,

Dull Knife's Cheyenne raiders at Dodge City on the steps of the courthouse. *Courtesy Kansas Historical Society.*

took them to court and fined them, and then released them. These fines, along with the license fees collected from saloonkeepers, paid the salaries of the town's peace officers.

The year 1879 saw no change as the spring months advanced. On April 5 there was a shootout in the Long Branch between Levi

Richardson, a freighter, and Frank Loving, a gambler. The two had been quarreling for some time, Richardson stating that he intended to "shoot the guts out of the cock-eyed son of a bitch." Both were contesting for the affections of the same woman. They met in the saloon on April 5, pulled revolvers, and started shooting. When it was over, Richardson was fatally wounded after eleven shots had been fired.[22] By June, when the cattlemen and cowboys arrived, Dodge was wide open. A typical good time that summer was described in the Ford County *Globe* on June 24: "The boys and girls across the dead line had a high old time last Friday. They sang and danced, and fought and bit, and cut and had a good time generally, making music for the entire settlement. Our reporter summed up five knock downs, three broken heads, two cuts and several incidental bruises. Unfortunately none of the injuries will prove fatal."

By the autumn of 1879 many residents of Dodge City were unhappy with the violence associated with their town, and there was strong talk of defeating Bat Masterson in his bid for reelection as sheriff that November. The editor of the Ford County *Globe* on September 16 indicated his support for George T. Hinkle, "who would make an excellent officer. He is not seeking the office, but would certainly make a strong candidate." The *Times* responded on October 25 that Bat Masterson "is acknowledged to be the best sheriff in Kansas." A majority of the voters apparently agreed with the editor of the *Globe*, for on November 4 they gave Hinkle 404 votes to Masterson's 268. The *Times* in its issue of November 8 hinted that the reform element had bought the election: "we conjecture the most powerful influence was in the beer keg; and of course people fighting for honesty and reform wouldn't use money." Masterson continued as sheriff until Hinkle took office in January 1880, after which he drifted west to join Wyatt Earp and his band of gambler-peace officer brothers and friends in Tombstone, Arizona.[23]

James Kelley and his cohorts in the Dodge City gang still controlled the mayor's office and the city council, and just after the election they appointed James Masterson the city marshal. For a time peace did reign between Hinkle and young Masterson, for Hinkle was by profession a bartender and saloonkeeper. Nor was feeling against the gang sufficiently high to sweep other gang members out of office. In the election in April 1880, Dr. Thomas L. McCarty, representing the reform element, was defeated by James Kelley, the gang member running for reelection as mayor. The editor of the *Globe* was angry at the result, writing "The polls were opened with twenty Kelley men on hand, each with blood in his eye, and only two or three to represent McCarty. . . . The Kelley men formed an almost solid phalanx around the polls, and it was only by a herculean effort that Christians could vote." The gang celebrated, but this was to be its last real victory.

The year 1880 was as free and open in Dodge City as in previous years. Cowboys arrived that summer and autumn to drink, gamble, consort with the prairie nymphs, and shoot up the town and each other. By March 1881 the situation had degenerated to the point where M. C. Ruby, an agent for the Adams Express Company office at Dodge, wrote a long exposé of affairs in the town; his charges were printed in the Oskaloosa, Iowa, *Herald*, on March 17, 1881. After asserting that the city attorney, Harry Gryden, had bragged that he would allow almost any charge to be dismissed for fifty to one hundred dollars, Ruby stated:

> The mayor is a flannel mouthed Irishman and keeps a saloon and gambling house which he attends to in person. The city marshal and assistant are gamblers and each keep a "woman"—as does the mayor also. The marshal and assistant for their services (as city officials) receive one hundred dollars per month, each. The sheriff [Hinkle] owns a saloon and the deputy sheriff [Fred Singer] is a bar tender in a saloon. . . . The ex-chairman of the Board of County Commissioners [A. J. Peacock] runs a saloon and dance hall, where the unwary are enticed, made drunk and robbed. Six men were knocked down and robbed one night last week. . . . There are many good people here, but the bad ones are so numerous we almost lose sight of the good. If any of your

readers anticipate immigrating to Kansas, advise them to shun Dodge City as they would the yellow fever, measles, smallpox and seven year itch combined, as I think they would all be preferable in a civilized county to residence in this town.

On April 4, 1881, when city elections were held, Mayor Kelley and the entire city council were defeated. A. B. Webster, the new mayor, within two days fired Jim Masterson and his assistant, Neil Brown, and appointed Fred Singer to the post. Singer had been under-sheriff to George Hinkle and was the bartender of the Old House saloon, which was owned by Mayor Webster. Tom Nixon, a former buffalo hunter, became the new assistant marshal. A few days later the new mayor posted his warning to members of the Dodge City gang: "To all whom it may concern: All thieves, thugs, confidence men, and persons without visible means of support, will take notice that the ordinance enacted for their special benefit will be rigorously enforced on and after tomorrow. April 7th, 1881. A. B. Webster, Mayor. Dodge City, Kansas."[24]

Almost immediately there was a quarrel that tested the mayor's resolve. Al Updegraph, the bartender at the Lady Gay, owned by Jim Masterson and A. J. Peacock, quarreled with Jim Masterson over the robbery of a woman by one of Masterson's friends. When Updegraph urged that charges be filed in the case, Masterson fired him as bartender and then threatened to kill him. Then, fearing reprisal, Masterson telegraphed his brother Bat, then at Tombstone, to come back and help him. Bat arrived on Friday morning, April 15, and the next day participated in a shootout in the streets of Dodge. On one side was Bat Masterson; on the other was Updegraph and A. J. Peacock. Casualties in the affair included Updegraph, shot through the lung, and windows in the Long Branch saloon, McCarty's drugstore, and George Hoover's wholesale liquor store. Mayor Webster and Fred Singer rushed in with shotguns and forced Masterson to surrender; later he was fined ten dollars plus court costs and allowed to leave town. Webster thereafter was known as the "fighting mayor." According to the Ford

County *Globe*, this shooting caused "great indignation" among local residents, for "the parties who were anxious to fight should have had at least a thought for the danger they were causing disinterested parties on the street and in business houses."[25] In August Masterson and Peacock sold the Lady Gay to Tom Nixon, the assistant town marshal, and O. A. "Brick" Bond, another former buffalo hunter.

Soon thereafter the mayor assumed almost total control over the saloon business in Dodge. He owned the Old House with the city marshal as its manager; the assistant marshal managed the Lady Gay, the city's only remaining dance hall. In November Mayor Webster leased what had been McCarty's drugstore and opened the Stock Exchange saloon, advertising it as a place to slake the thirst, exhilarate the mind, and "brace up" a weak constitution. He collected money from other saloonkeepers, gamblers, and prostitutes in the form of licenses and fines; these funds were used to pay the costs of law enforcement. Webster did not want to end immorality in Dodge, only to control it—and to share in its profits.

By the spring of 1882, definite changes were evident in the town. A temperance society had been formed in the Union Church. New homes were being constructed, and there was talk of paving the principal streets in town. The Santa Fe had three passenger trains daily in each direction, and its management was talking of a new depot. Henry Sturm sold soda pop—strawberry, raspberry, ginger ale, lemon, and vanilla—in his liquor store, and George Hoover added drugs to his line of liquor, for he claimed that he was selling alcoholic beverages only for medicinal purposes. Finally came the wearing of police uniforms by the city marshal and his officers. Commented the editor of the *Times* on July 13, 1882, "There is a metropolitan air in their manner." With these came new police regulations from the mayor's office that required officers to devote their whole time to the business of the department; they had to be civil, orderly, sober, and discreet.[26]

Because of these new regulations, Marshal Fred Singer resigned in June to devote his energies to operating the Old House saloon. He was replaced by Jack Bridges, a former United States Deputy Marshal. Dodge proved remarkably quiet during 1882. Such was not to be the case the following year, however.

The Ford County *Globe* on February 6, 1883, carried a notice that Chalk Beeson had sold his interest in the Long Branch saloon to Luke L. Short, who would continue as a partner of W. H. Harris. Short had arrived in Dodge in August 1882. He was a gambler who dressed the part with diamond tie pin, elegantly flashy clothes, mustache, gold-headed walking cane; and he had great skill with a pistol. Almost immediately after Short purchased an interest in the Long Branch his partner, W. H. Harris, became the Dodge City gang's candidate for mayor. By this time the Ford County *Globe* had changed sides and was supporting the gang and its candidates. Nicholas B. Klaine's Dodge City *Times* likewise had shifted, throwing its support to the reform element, whose candidate for mayor was former city marshal Larry Deger. When the votes were counted on April 3, Deger had 214 votes, Harris 143.

Three weeks later the reformers in the city government passed Ordinance No. 70; its purpose, according to its title, was "the suppression of vice and immorality within the city of Dodge City." This provided stiff fines for prostitutes and the keepers of brothels. Ordinance No. 71, passed at the same time, was "to define and punish vagrancy" and was intended to hasten the departure from town of "any person who may be found loitering around houses of ill-fame, gambling houses, or places where liquors are sold or drank, without any visible means of support or lawful vocation."

Two days later, Saturday, April 28, with extra police added to the force, arrests were made of "singers" in the Long Branch saloon. Short and Harris were outraged, claiming "that partiality was shown" by the arrest of women in their establishment but not those in the Old House, the Lone Star, the Opera House, or the Lady Gay. Short, whose temper matched his name, immediately went to the home of Fred Wenie, the city attorney, roused him

Luke Short. *Courtesy Kansas Historical Society.*

from bed, and at pistol point secured bonds for the release of his girls. Later that evening Short encountered Louis C. Hartman, the city clerk who was one of the extra policemen hired and who had arrested Short's singers. The two exchanged gun shots, but neither was hit. Hartman then swore out a complaint against Short, Marshal Bridges arrested him, and Short had to post a bond of $2000. Commented the Dodge City *Times* in its issue of May 3 about the incident, "Mayor Deger is a resolute, fearless and obstinate officer. All good and law abiding citizens are standing by him in this trying emergency."

Indeed a group of citizens had formed around Deger and Marshal Bridges, a group that constituted a vigilante force. With warrants sworn out, the vigilantes arrested Short and six of his friends, described in the *Times* as "a former New Mexico desperado," four gamblers, and a saloonkeeper. All were held in jail and then placed on a train; their only choice was to take the eastbound or the westbound. Short went to Kansas City to rally support. Two of the gamblers attempted to return, but as they descended from the train they were met by the vigilantes, pistols in hand, and decided to leave again.

Despite George Hoover's advice by letter to sell the Long Branch, Short journeyed to Topeka to meet with Governor George W. Glick, a known antiprohibitionist. Short complained to the governor that his arrest and removal from town stemmed from "political differences and Business rivalry," and he said he wanted protection from "the unlawful violence" of his enemies.[27] Glick responded by alerting two companies of state national guardsmen, one at Sterling and another at Newton; they were to stand in readiness to move into Dodge City should the situation deteriorate. Sheriff George Hinkle, when queried about the incident by telegram, told the governor that Short had been forced to leave; Hinkle wanted to stay neutral. To counteract this statement, twelve of Dodge City's leading businessmen journeyed to Topeka to say that Short was lying and that no state interference was needed in their city.[28]

At this point Short telegraphed such former Dodge gamblers and saloonkeepers as Bat Masterson, Doc Holliday, Wyatt Earp, Rowdy Joe Lowe, and "Shortgun" Collins. He wanted staunch allies if the issue was to be settled with bullets. When this word spread in Dodge, Sheriff Hinkle deputized a posse of forty-five men to search all trains arriving from the East. A war of serious proportions seemed about to begin. So worried were some local businessmen by these events that Robert Wright, Chalk Beeson, and George Hoover journeyed to Kansas City to talk with Short to try to effect a compromise. Meanwhile, both sides were bombarding editors with letters explaining the "true" state of affairs in Dodge City.

Governor Glick was so anxious to learn the truth that he sent Adjutant General Thomas Moonlight to Dodge to make a personal inspection. Moonlight successfully persuaded Mayor Deger to allow Short to return within ten days to settle his affairs. Moonlight then returned to Topeka, but at the end of ten days Short had not returned to Dodge. On May 31 Wyatt Earp and Doc Holliday arrived, followed on June 3 by Short and on June 4 by Bat Masterson. By Wednesday the city fathers were so worried that they telegraphed the governor, "Our city is overrun with desperate characters from Colorado, New Mexico, Arizona and California. We cannot preserve the peace or enforce the laws. Will you send in two companies of militia at once to assist us in preserving the peace between all parties and enforcing the laws." The governor responded by sending Adjutant General Moonlight back to Dodge.

Twenty minutes after Moonlight got on the train for Dodge, another telegram arrived at the governor's office. Sheriff Hinkle wired, "The difficulty is all settled. Short's fighters have left town. I am satisfied we will not have any more trouble." A compromise had been reached between the two factions allowing gambling to take place in the city provided it occurred in a section of the saloon partitioned off from the barroom and dance hall. Women could frequent saloons, but under more discreet circumstances than pre-

The famed "Dodge City Peace Commission" of 1883. In the back row, left to right, are W. H. Harris, Luke Short, Bat Masterson, and W. F. Petillon; in the front row are Charles Bassett, Wyatt Earp, M. F. McLain, and Neal Brown. *Courtesy Kansas Historical Society.*

viously, and Short and his friends promised to help rid the town of some of the more crooked gamblers and confidence men. Just before Short's "army" left town, the members gathered for a photograph, the eight men calling themselves the "Dodge City Peace Commission." After peace reigned for several months, Short and Harris sold the Long Branch to Roy Drake and Frank Warren on November 19, 1883.[29]

It was well that they left, for Dodge City definitely was changing. By September that year a city ordinance forced all businesses to close on Sunday, although the post office, the drugstore, and the butcher shop could do business for one hour. Dodge was becoming civilized. Along with the closing law came another city ordinance banning music and singing in dance halls and saloons, leading one wit to send a poem to the editor of the *Times* concerning the Lady Gay dance hall, owned by Tom Nixon and Brick Bond:

> I have wandered to the Dance Hall, Tom,
>   Where in the days gone by,
> We tripped the light fantastic toe,
>   Together, you and I.
> The same old "brick" is in the hall—
>   But the "bells" "swing" not to and fro—
> The music is not the same, dear Tom,
>   As it was a few days ago.[30]

In the election in the fall of 1883, Patrick F. Sughrue was elected sheriff, while George M. Hoover was chosen mayor on April 7, 1884. Both appear to have been compromise candidates, nodding toward reform but not shutting the saloons or prohibiting prostitution altogether. Drunken cowboys continued to shoot up the town late at night as they celebrated reaching the end of the trail. Hoover's choice for town marshal was William M. Tilghman, Jr., who, with Henry Garis, had owned and operated the Crystal Palace and Oasis saloons for a time. Tilghman had been serving as a deputy to Sheriff Sughrue and, after his appointment by Mayor Hoover, chose Tom Nixon as his assistant marshal, replacing Mysterious Dave Mather, who had been serving as assistant to Jack Bridges.

Mather and Nixon became bitter enemies over this affair. On July 18 Nixon shot at the former assistant marshal, claiming that Mather had drawn first. Sheriff Sughrue disarmed and arrested Nixon, who posted a bond of $800 and was released. Three days later, according to the report in the *Glove Live Stock Journal*, "Nixon was on duty at the corner of Front Street and First Avenue" when Mather, "who keeps a saloon in the Opera House, came down stairs and deliberately shot him through." Nixon was dead where he fell, and a nearby cowboy was wounded by one of the bullets which passed through Nixon's body and hit the cowboy in the leg. After the shooting and before his arrest, Mather calmly stated, "I ought to have killed him six months ago." At his subsequent trial Mather was acquitted and released.[31]

By 1885, however, the boom period was ending—and with it the gunfighting, gambling, prostitution, and fist fighting that had characterized Dodge City. Several factors in combination forced the city to become what several editors had been demanding for years: civilized.

The March of Civilization

In 1882 Nicholas B. Klaine, editor of one of the local newspapers and a deacon in one of the churches, spoke to the Literary Union Society, a new organization in town. Klaine held out hope for the future, asserting, "The city's rude and uncouth character is the indication of a polished and established future. As the homely child becomes a handsome man, so will Dodge, born of ugliness and roughness, mature in brightness and smoothness."[1] Thoughtful members in his audience already could see that their town was changing from the old, carefree town into something resembling stable communities to the east, for the buffalo hunter and soldier already were a part of the past by 1882.

Fort Dodge had been founded to contain the restless plains tribes of nomadic Indians. During the early 1870s soldiers from Fort Dodge had regularly marched out in pursuit of Comanche, Kiowa, and Kiowa-Apache renegades, and General Nelson A. Miles had taken a detachment of troops south from Fort Dodge to participate in the Red River war of 1874-1875 that brought the final containment of these tribes on reservations in the Indian Territory. After 1875 the soldiers at Fort Dodge occasionally were called out to pursue some small party of renegades, but the majority of Indians no longer had any will to fight. Thus the troops settled into routine patrols, escorting wagon trains, and maintaining the peace between ranchers and farmers. In 1878 there was a brief flurry of activity when Chief Dull Knife and his Cheyenne warriors attempted to leave the Indian Territory and return to their traditional mountain home to the northwest. Troops from Dodge aided in forcing a Cheyenne surrender.

By 1878, however, General John Pope, commander of the division, suggested that Fort Dodge be closed.[2] Pope's recommendation found favor in Kansas where homesteaders wanted to stake a claim on the land within the military reservation. In 1879 Congress passed a law opening the northern two-thirds of the land belonging to Fort Dodge to settlement, but the Department of the Interior challenged the law. This was overruled, and on December 15, 1880, the land was thrown open. Those filing for this acreage included only ten settlers, including four widows; the others were prostitutes, gamblers, saloonkeepers, and railroad employees. The rest of the land within the military reservation was opened in 1889 with a "run" similar to the one held in Oklahoma that year.[3] Orders to close Fort Dodge itself were issued on April 5, 1882. Everything portable was removed to Camp Supply in the Indian Territory, and on October 2 that year the flag was lowered for the final time, and the buildings were turned over to a caretaker hired by the War Department.

The first caretaker, James Langton, lasted only a year before he grew bored and retired. Next was Robert M. Wright, former sutler at the post and a merchant in Dodge City. Wright had used the profits from his business ventures to invest in ranch land near the fort, and he sought the position of caretaker to further his own scheme—using the buildings at Fort Dodge to house cattle drovers and their herds while they awaited the sale of their animals in Dodge City. Then in 1886 some of the former officers' quarters were used to house the victims of a smallpox outbreak. In 1889 the remaining land on the reservation was thrown open to settlement, and the buildings were turned over to the Department of the Interior.[4]

Several Kansans had thoughts about some new use for the buildings at Fort Dodge. For a time there was talk of turning these quarters into a school for Indian children. Then the Methodist College Association of southwestern Kansas petitioned for permission to purchase the buildings as housing for a college. However, the legislature in Kansas requested that Congress turn over the buildings to the state to be used as a home for aged soldiers from Kansas; the cost was $1.25 per acre. The residents of Dodge City collected the money, made the purchase, and readied the place for occupancy on January 1, 1890. Qualifications for admission were residence in Kansas for two years, military service in one of the nation's wars, and financial need. Single residents were housed in the enlisted men's barracks, while those with families were quartered in the former officers' houses. Most of the first successful applicants were elderly veterans of the Civil War who wanted to carry firearms (still permitted by Kansas law), and most were inclined to go into town and get drunk. The first Confederate veterans were admitted in 1900, and the first black veteran in 1912. Today approximately 400 veterans still live at the old post.[5]

The end of the buffalo had come shortly after the Army in 1875 forced the Indians onto permanent reservations. That summer the hunters swarmed across the plains doing their work in methodical fashion. The slaughter was completed by 1878 on the southern herd, leaving only carcasses which wolves and buzzards quickly picked clean. Some places, where a hunter had made a stand and had killed hundreds of buffalo, piles of bones covered the plains and turned them white. Those people marking wagon roads did so with piles of these bones. However, these bones did not long remain, for inventive Americans soon found a use for them.

New bones were found useful in refining sugar, for the calcium phosphate in them neutralized the acid in cane juice. Old, weathered bones could be ground into a meal and used as fertilizer, for they consisted of calcium that enriched the soil. A few choice bones could be made into bone china, and horns had value for making buttons, combs, and knife handles. Buyers therefore

Bone piles and workmen curing buffalo hides at Dodge. *Courtesy Kansas Historical Society.*

moved into Dodge City with the coming of the railroad, buying bones for $2.50 to $3.00 per ton and horns for $6.00 to $8.00 per ton. Enterprising citizens soon learned that these bones were to be had free by a man with a wagon and a willingness to drive across the plains loading it; a hard-working man could make as much as, if not more than the hunters and skinners. In fact, Dodge City became the headquarters for the bone trade in southwestern Kansas, and piles of them could be seen for miles east of town, waiting for freight cars to be available on the Santa Fe to take them to St. Louis, which became the major point for manufacturing them into a useful product. Because the air was dry around Dodge, bones did not weigh much and it took a large pile of them to make a ton; this caused some bone hunters to wet down the bones and make them weigh more. Major Richard I. Dodge, while commanding the fort just outside the town, estimated that in 1872 the Santa Fe Railroad alone shipped 1,135,300 pounds of bones, the following year 2,743,100 pounds, and in 1874 an astonishing 6,914,950 pounds. He figured that the Santa Fe hauled about one-third of all bones being shipped east, making 32,380,050 pounds for the three years.[6] By 1880, however, the bone trade was largely over. Dodge City's future was totally committed to the Texas cattle trade and catering to the needs of the cowboy when he arrived in town with money in his pocket.

Three elements were inextricably linked as Dodge changed from a wide-open town at the end of a cattle trail to a stable Kansas community: the state quarantine law (east of which cattle could not be driven), the advancing farmers' frontier, and the enforcement of state and city laws concerning alcoholic beverages and prostitution. Moral reform came only when the city's businessmen no longer were dependent on the cattle trade for a majority of their income, and the cattlemen ceased coming only when the farmers in Ford County increased in number until they could persuade the legislature to close the area to Texas cattle.

In fact, it was a moving of the quarantine line westward in 1876 that ended Wichita as a cattle center and allowed Dodge to boom. Then in 1877 another legislative enactment moved the so-called deadline out to the eastern edge of Ford County.[7] Almost immediately there was agitation from farmers in the northeastern corner of Ford County to close the entire county to the Texas cattle trade, for splenic (or Texas) fever was killing their domestic cows. An informal agreement between these farmers and those in the cattle trade protected their area, and nothing came of their petition that year. In 1877 rainfall at Dodge totaled 27.9 inches, leading to a large migration of farmers to the area—and an increase in demands for closing the area to cattle in 1878. However, 1878 proved dry, with just 18.0 inches of rain, and 1879 proved even drier with only 15.4 inches; in 1880 rainfall totaled 18.1 inches. Thus from 1878 to 1881 the number of farmers in Ford County declined somewhat; those who remained were at the raw edge of poverty. A reporter visiting the county in January 1880 commented:

In the east end of the county there is want, privation and suffering, and in the west [at Dodge City] there is waste, extravagance,
dissipation and licentiousness. The money spent foolishly in the
"Famous City" in one week would be sufficient to keep the poor
of the county for the entire winter. But the good work goes on.
Those who spend foolishly continue to do so and the hungry ones
are still hungry.[8]

The Dodge City *Times*, a staunch supporter of the cattle trade,
railed against any relief for these drought-stricken farmers, but in
February 1880 the county commissioners purchased 7500 pounds
of cornmeal, 3000 pounds of flour, and 500 pounds of bacon for
distribution to them, while the Dodge City Benevolent Society
spent all its funds for aid to the suffering farmers.[9] Many residents
of Dodge City were not unhappy with this drought; "Damn the
grangers," one of them wrote in 1878, "I wish it wouldn't rain this
summer so that they would starve out."[10]

During this dry era the gang in Dodge City was able to retain
almost total control of the town, and gang members could ignore
prohibition laws passed at the state level. In November 1880 a
constitutional amendment establishing prohibition was passed by
the voters of the state, and the legislature enacted laws to enforce
it beginning on May 1, 1881. In Dodge City the law was totally
ignored, for no local law enforcement official believed in it, nor did
courts, businessmen, and most town residents. Bob Wright served
Ford County in the legislature and managed to secure the chairmanship of the committee handling the issue of the quarantine
law; as a leading businessman in Dodge, he managed to kill any
measure to move the deadline west. He was succeeded in 1883 by
George M. Hoover who won the same committee chairmanship
and kept Ford County exempt; even in 1884, when a special session of the legislature was called to halt an outbreak of hoof-and-
mouth disease, Hoover kept Ford County open to Texas cattle.

Because of these developments, several residents of the county,
as well as outsiders, began ranching in the area. Some Texas cattlemen had occupied empty land south and west of Dodge as early

as 1876, and on these they held over for fattening cattle that did not sell at high prices that year. By 1878 the Ford County *Globe* regularly published livestock brands of local ranchers. Those animals that for one reason or another did not sell to the packing companies could be bought in the fall for very little money; these would be turned loose to fend for themselves during the winter, and those that lived would quickly fatten on the lush spring grass and sell far better than the gaunt animals just arriving up the trail from Texas. By 1882, when prices for beef were high, George Hoover, Herman Fringer, Bob Wright, and many other Dodge residents had invested in this trade. As early as 1878 editor Nicholas Klaine had commented, "The cattle trade of this town, in a measure, is being localized, by the establishment of cattle camps and ranches on the broad plain. This insures a permanency and establishes a local trade that will meet with no fluctuations."[11]

In 1882 cattle shipments at Dodge were more than double those of the previous year, and profits by local merchants were correspondingly high. This led, in April 1883, to the formation at Dodge of the Western Kansas Cattle Growers' Association, with its headquarters in Bob Wright's store. This further tied local businessmen and the ranchers together. In fact, by 1884 local ranching had grown to the point that those engaged in it no longer were as happy with the cattle drives coming up from Texas. The ticks were killed on cattle wintering in Kansas, and the arrival of new herds from the south reinfested the whole herd. Meeting in Dodge in 1884, members of the Association called for an end to the summer drives up from Texas. They were aided by two circumstances that summer: slumping prices for cattle, and an outbreak of splenic fever in stockyards in Chicago and Kansas City. When the governor of Illinois threatened to keep out all cattle shipped from Kansas, Governor George W. Glick summarily cut off all further imports of Texas cattle on August 13. Already an estimated 300,600 head of longhorns had arrived at Dodge by this time; thereafter Sheriff Patrick Sughrue tried to halt further drives.

Local ranchers wanting to halt the drives were joined by local farmers, who had increased rapidly beginning with a wet cycle in 1881. Between 1882 and 1884 the population of Ford County almost doubled. These were people who wanted the prohibition laws enforced, the houses of prostitution closed, and the cattle trade ended. They joined to elect a reform ticket in 1881 and again in 1883. However, A.B. Webster, elected mayor in 1881, chose to compromise, for he was a businessman who did not want *radical* reform. Larry Deger, who succeeded Webster in 1883, enforced the laws selectively, triggering the saloon war with Luke Short. In August that year, when the reformers wanted to abolish gambling, the major businessmen insisted on business as usual and nothing was done.

In 1884, elections in Dodge City were largely fought over the issue of prohibition. Editor Klaine had made the *Times* an organ for the Republican drys, while Daniel M. Frost, editor of the *Globe*, championed the Republican wet cause. The Democrats by this time had their own paper, the Dodge City *Democrat*; many of its constituents were recently arrived Germans who believed they should have their beer, and thus the *Democrat* urged a wet vote. A. B. Webster, leader of the moderate businessmen in town, saw a need for alcoholic beverages for Texas cowboys coming to Dodge and led his faction in voting wet. The result was the reelection of George M. Hoover for mayor, along with Jim Kelley on the city council. The wet slate defeated the dry by a wide majority of more than four to one. Klaine philosophically editorialized, "The city election would indicate that the people of Dodge were not ready for reform."[12]

A year later the same coalition of wets elected Bob Wright mayor of Dodge City, and the saloons, gambling halls, and dance halls were open and ready to greet the cowboys when they arrived. But for a time it seemed there might be none coming north. The state legislature in February passed an embargo on all cattle originating in south and central Texas—the area afflicted with splenic fever. Klaine responded under a story titled, "No more Texas Cattle to Dodge City."[13] However, the law did allow these cattle to enter the state after December 1, by which time the cold climate would have killed all ticks. Texans still brought their cattle north despite the law—only to find few buyers along with angry farmers in their path. Local ranchers, who had been using the public range to graze their cattle, saw their land overrun that year by sodbusters, and they began shipping their animals into the Oklahoma Panhandle, the Texas Panhandle, or southern Colorado. Dan Frost wrote on December 1, 1885, "Yes, our ranges have passed into history."[14]

Suddenly in Dodge City the farmer, who for years had been scorned as "grangers" and cheapskates, was recognized as the economic wave of the future. In August 1885 Frost wrote, "Farmers are the producers that supply our tables, and there is no class of people that the world would rather see prosper than the farmer. . . . Good times on the farm means good times in town."[15] Samuel S. Prouty, editor of the Dodge City *Cowboy*, gave an even greater indication of surrender to the new order, stating that "Western Kansas is now blooming and blooming." On October 3, 1885, he stated:

> The experience of all cattle towns is that their growth had been held in check during the period when they depended upon the cattle trade for support. The country surrounding could not be developed while it was being held for stock ranges. Abilene, Wichita, Newton, Ellsworth and Great Bend . . . all shot ahead with amazing rapidity when the cattle business left them. Dodge City has been for the past ten years an exclusive cattle town. The cattle traffic made money for its citizens but did not make a town. . . . The rains of the past three years, the assurance that the soil of the country is susceptible of successful cultivation, the recent absorption of the public domain by settlers, the removal of the cattle trail and the rapidly disappearing cowboy, have now thoroughly convinced our people that a permanent commercial metropolis at this point is demanded by the needs of the country.

These changes also spelled the end of the saloon and the brothel in Dodge. In February 1885 the legislature in Kansas strengthened the prohibition law by enacting a provision allowing any citizen to seek an injunction against a saloon where the city or county attorney failed to take action, and when a private citizen engaged an attorney for the purpose of closing a saloon that attorney could act in the place of the county attorney. This act forced several Dodge liquor dealers, such as George Hoover, to sell out. Thereafter only bootleggers, those willing to risk fine and imprisonment, and druggists sold whiskey, the latter for "medical, scientific, and mechanical purposes." One store erected a sign stating, "Drug Store. Lager Beer on Ice, for Medical Purposes only."[16] A. B. Webster and his partner Brick Bond changed the title of the Stock Exchange to drugstore, while William H. Harris and his partner Roy Drake announced, "The Long Branch Temperance Hall has opened up . . . with such old-time lemonade and temperance drink mixers as Edward Cooley and Moses Barber, who are both gentlemanly fellows and know how to entertain their numerous customers."[17] Under these new names the saloons were as active as ever.

In June Albert Griffin, an organizer for the Kansas State Temperance Union, arrived in Dodge to found a chapter, which drew sixty charter members. On June 25 he filed an injunction against local liquor dealers, but found the county attorney unwilling to prosecute. Therefore he hurried to the state capital to urge Attorney General S. B. Bradford to come to Dodge and see how the law was being flouted. Bradford did send a deputy with Griffin, but at Dodge on June 29 the two men were manhandled by an angry mob and fled town the next morning. Griffin then begged Governor John A. Martin to send in the militia to clean up Dodge, but the governor chose to listen to District Court Judge Jeremiah C. Strong of Dodge City, who wrote:

> The quarantine law passed last winter is quietly working out the salvation of Dodge City. The festive cowboy is already becoming conspicuous by his absence in Dodge, and ere long he will be seen & heard there, in his glory, no more forever. The cowboy gone the gamblers and prostitutes will find their occupations gone, and,

from necessity, must follow. The bulk of the saloons will then die out because there will be no sufficient support left, and the temperance people can close the rest as easily as they could in any other city in Kansas.

The governor sent Attorney General Bradford to Dodge, and he agreed with Judge Strong's assessment.[18]

In October, however, a gambler under indictment in Edwards County fled to Dodge City, and when an Edwards County deputy came to arrest him the deputy was forced by a mob to leave town empty-handed. Governor Martin thereupon wrote Mayor Bob Wright, "Sooner or later, you know that Dodge must reform or perish. Why not reform it now? Why cannot all decent citizens of Dodge unite in a determined effort to make Dodge an orderly, peacable [sic], decent and prosperous city?" Wright replied in the old manner, arguing that the complaints were made by a few "soreheads" who "breed all the trouble here & continually keep things in hot water." These people, he said, "are public disturbers & are a curse to any community—who want every one to think & do as they say—who if they cant rule want to ruin, who do not hesitate to lie & prevaricate to gain their selfish ends, who pretend to be Moralists but are wolves in sheeps clothing." He concluded by saying Dodge was different from other communities in that it was "a frontier Town, where the wild & reckless sons of the Plains have congregated."[19]

The situation came to a head in the county elections in November 1885. Thanks to a large majority in the Dodge City precinct, plus the wets in both Democratic and Republican parties supporting what they called the "People's Ticket," the wets won by a slim margin. The reform element swore that fraud had been committed and on November 24 filed suit in the state supreme court to disallow the ballots from Dodge City.[20] That same day Attorney General Bradford came to Dodge to close the saloons he had been told were operating, but he found them closed. The locals had heard he was coming and locked everything up; the day after Bradford left town they were open again.

That night, November 27, the first of Dodge City's two major fires occurred. In January the *Kansas Cowboy*, a newspaper then published in Dodge City, had asserted that the town was "a little paradise for fire insurance companies," for the city had never had "any fires in the city, involving loss to insurance companies." This the paper attributed to the fact that "many of its business houses are never closed; its saloons are frequented by people at all hours, and at no time, day or night, are the streets destitute of pedestrians. . . ." Thus any fire that broke out was discovered in its infancy and put out. The next day a minor fire started in a grocery store on Front Street and spread to the office of the *Kansas Cowboy*, destroying it along with half a block of property and some warehouses south of the railroad tracks.

The fire in November was far worse. Apparently it began when an oil lamp either exploded or was dropped, and it quickly spread, consuming everything between Bob Wright's store and Jim Kelley's Opera House. This was the heart of the business district. Rumors spread quickly that the fire was the work of prohibitionists because of the many saloons destroyed. The fire caused additional anger because during it Bob Wright had fired three shots from his pistol into the house owned by Mike Sutton, a leading prohibitionist. Later he claimed he had seen a prowler and was shooting at him, but Sutton believed Wright had intended to murder him. The *Globe's* account of the fire stated, "By an over sight some awful good whiskey was allowed to burn up." There was some looting; of the few arrested for this crime, the *Times* stated, "A man who would steal under such circumstances ought to be stretched in stocks and slowly kicked to death by grasshoppers."

Within hours after the fire ended, the old spirit that had led to the founding of the town was evident. Delmonico's restaurant opened in a vacant building, and Bob Wright contracted for a temporary building beside the ruins of his old brick establishment. Other businesses operating out of temporary quarters naturally included several saloons as some men drank to forget the $150,000 loss caused by the fire.

Just ten days later a second major fire started at midnight in a house of prostitution just north of the central block of Front Street. A prostitute known as "Sawed-off" had sent a bootblack to warm her room; he started a fire and left; shortly afterward a pedestrian saw fire coming through the roof. It spread quickly, engulfing several stores and new offices of the *Kansas Cowboy*. When the flames died, yet another city block in Dodge had been leveled.

As this fire raged, a signal flag was flying on the court house flag pole, the signal used by the local weather bureau to indicate a blizzard about to hit. It hit on New Year's day, 1886, the temperature well below zero. There followed the worst storm since 1872, the year Dodge was founded. An estimated half to three-quarters of the cattle in the county died, while the new farmers in the county, most of them living in clapboard shanties or soddies, were "overtaken by these severe storms with little or no fuel and scanty supply of provisions," according to the Dodge City *Democrat*. Before the snows of the first storm melted, a second hit on the evening of January 13 compounding the agony.

As a result of fire and ice, Dodge City entered a period of depression. Businessmen in the city had been wiped out by the fire, many of them without insurance, and those who had invested their surplus capital in cattle saw these herds sadly depleted. Bob Wright had to sell 7000 acres of his land to pay his taxes; John Mueller, a boot maker, grew so discouraged that he left town; Jim Kelley, the former mayor, rebuilt his Opera House at a cost of $20,000, but sold it in 1898 to Adolphus Gluck, a jeweler, for $3800.[21]

Compounding the misery was the winter of 1886-1887, probably the most severe ever experienced on the Great Plains. The storms came early that fall. A warm wind that blew up from the south in January, melting snow and raising hopes, was immediately followed by a howling blizzard. Cattle, driven by a merciless wind, piled up against fences and died by the thousands. A numbing cold followed the storm, and the thermometer dropped dramatically. Cowboys, imprisoned for weeks around bunkhouse stoves, dared not think of the starving, freezing herds, unable to find food or shelter.

When spring finally came in 1887, cattlemen and cowboys were greeted by a sight that many spent the rest of their lives trying to forget: carcass piled atop carcass, gaunt cattle staggering about on frozen feet, and trees stripped bare of their bark by starving animals. Losses across the county were estimated at 66 percent, and many ranchers were bankrupted. When the snow finally melted that spring, the grass came back as good as ever, but cattlemen had lost their unshakable belief that money could be made by ranching. Ford County became farm country. At first this seemed a blessing. In March 1885 the population of Dodge City was 1402; a year later it moved from a third-class to a second-class city, for proof had been furnished the governor that it had 2000 residents.

Unfortunately for Dodge City's reputation as "the wickedest city in America," the farmers were inclined to inhabit churches and schools more than saloons and dance halls, and soon the city became little more than a copy of other county seat towns in Kansas. Nor were the farmers as generous with their money as had been the cowboys coming up from Texas; in fact, few of these farmers had any money to spend wildly on whiskey, women, and gambling. Despite the machinery helping to ease their physical burdens, many of these farmers had come onto the Great Plains armed only with the courage of ignorance. They planted corn but found it would grow only in years of high rainfall. They tried barley, sorghum, and millet, but with only limited success. Finally wheat became the staple crop, but in dry years serious failures occurred. Summers were made hot by dry winds from the south that parched crops in their path, while the blizzards of winter killed farm animals. Recurring droughts turned much of the region into a desert, and grasshopper plagues filled the prairie farmer's cup of frustrations. These grasshoppers, according to one farmer, ate everything but the mortgage. Wagons could be seen leaving Ford County in the autumn of bad years with a sign painted on the side: "In God we trusted; in Kansas we busted."

One serious attempt was made to prevent the ravages of drought by digging a canal to provide water for irrigation. Asa T. Soule, a visionary with a dream of founding a Utopia, came to Ford

County in 1883 after making a fortune selling patent medicine in Rochester, New York. In Dodge he invested in a national bank, and he built the Dodge City, Montezuma, and Trinidad Railroad (later abandoned as economically unsound). Moreover, he donated land and $50,000 to build a Presbyterian college, named Soule in his honor, on the north side of Dodge; it opened in 1888 (but was sold to the Methodists in 1893 when financial disaster overtook it; in 1912 the Catholics transformed it into a girls' school, Saint Mary of the Plains).

In addition, Soule established the Eureka Irrigation Canal Company in 1883 to take water from the Arkansas River and divert it to farm use. About twenty miles upriver from Dodge City, he established a town at first bearing his name; but very shortly after its founding he saw political advantage in renaming it Ingalls (for United States Senator John J. Ingalls of Kansas, famous for his statement that "Kansas is the navel of the nation"). Employing hundreds of men, along with horses and plows, the Eureka Irrigation Canal Company constructed a canal which ran from Ingalls and reached the community of Spearville some twenty miles northeast of Dodge City. The work took four years. After completion in 1888 water flowed into fields at Spearville and ended fear of drought there. Shortly before his death in 1890, Soule sold his stock in the Eureka to a group of English investors for $1,100,000. His heirs no doubt appreciated his foresight, for early in the 20th century the canal went dry because so many other irrigation projects had been constructed along the Arkansas and because drought lowered the level of the river.[22]

Dodge City's fortunes and appearance thus changed drastically in the mid-1880s. Its future was tied to waving fields of wheat, and soon grain elevators and even a flour mill could be seen above other buildings in town. Dodge was facing a future no different from that of a hundred other towns in southwestern Kansas— except for the memories associated with its wild and easy period. Thanks to these, its future was altered.

Gunsmoke Returns to Dodge

Dodge City was among the last of the wide-open frontier towns in the American West, a contemporary of Tombstone, Arizona, and Deadwood, South Dakota. All three achieved a bad reputation while they were still young for having few civilized restraints on exuberant young men who worked hard, who had an intimate acquaintance with danger, and who arrived in town with money in their pockets and a lusty appetite for a wild spree. The mountain man, the Santa Fe Trader, the Forty Niner—who preceded the cowboy and the buffalo hunter on the frontier—would have recognized and appreciated the attitude in these three towns, for they catered to the needs and desires of men freed from the restraining influences of wives and sweethearts, of religious and social pressures, even of economic dependency on bosses and creditors. Here the young cowboy, miner, and buffalo hunter could scratch where he itched, belch without embarrassment, dress in what he found comfortable, get drunk when the urge struck, make fun of pretense and culture, and quit any job he found distasteful.

Theirs was a wild kind of freedom that had strong appeal to people living in Eastern cities where squalid social and economic conditions caused residents to long, secretly or openly, for escape. Journalists of that day understood the frustrations of their big-city

readers, and in writing about these towns in the West they indulged in wild exaggeration. Drinking became alcoholism, prostitutes and dance hall girls became nymphs whose desire was to
satisfy men and who had hearts of gold, shootings involved brave
men triumphing over the forces of evil, and freedom became
irresponsibility.

Of the three wide-open cities of the 1870s, Dodge City assumed
a unique position, for the transients coming there were cowboys,
not miners, and the romantic legend of the young man on horseback, living an independent life under the prairie stars, full of
swagger and bluster, carrying a gun, dealing in life and death, already had become an indelible part of American folklore. George
Ward Nichols of *Harper's Magazine*, along with a host of writers
and journalists, had fanned across the West, believing what they
wanted and making up the rest to produce a picture of Buffalo
Bill, James Butler "Wild Bill" Hickok, and Jesse James as the
equivalents of Achilles, King David, and Lancelot. They portrayed
these third-rate characters as knights and Robin Hoods whose
swords were Colt .45s, and whose armor was their ability to out-
draw and outshoot their rivals. These mythical heroes found enjoyment in cards, but seldom drank; they were modest; they were kind
to women, no matter what their age or beauty; they were prodi-
giously accurate with firearms, handsome, and blue-eyed. In short,
the Western hero became a stock character, a pasteboard hero,
participating in a morality play about good triumphing over evil.
For example, E. C. Little entitled an article in *Everybody's Magazine* in 1902, "Round Table of Dodge City: Border Men, Knights-
Errant Who Surpassed the Achievements of Heroes of Romance."

The old-timers of Dodge City, along with second-generation
residents and newcomers, wanted no part in such nonsense as they
battled into the 20th century, fighting nature to wrest a livelihood
from farms, ranches, and supporting businesses in town. Unlike
Tombstone and Deadwood, Dodge, when the historic reason for
its founding no longer existed, still had fertile soil surrounding it,
land that would grow grass to feed cattle or on which wheat could

be raised. Thus the town grew slowly as the county seat of Ford County and as a supply and distribution point for the farmers and ranchers in the vicinity. Major events no longer were gunfights and the threat of martial law; rather the people celebrated the dedication of a new county courthouse which opened in 1913 at a cost of $100,000, of a country club in 1917, and the new city hall in 1929. And they saw change come as Ham Bell switched from operating a livery stable to running an automobile agency, and as Bob Wright's store became the home of a nickel and dime national chain store. They saw the opening of a Red Cross canteen at the Santa Fe depot and the building of a victory arch at the corner of Second Avenue and Walnut Street when the boys came home from France in 1918. World War II was brought closer to home to them when Dodge City Air Field opened there, and they participated in rationing, opened a USO canteen for servicemen, and read casualty lists to see if local boys' names were on them. But these were elements Dodge shared with other towns in Kansas and the United States.

During the early years of the 20th century residents deliberately wanted to forget the violence that marked the beginning of their town. In 1910, for example, Jess C. Denious came to Dodge as the new owner of the *Globe*. A young newspaperman, he was enthralled as he read through the back files of his paper and he reprinted some of the articles about bad men and dark deeds. Several prominent citizens immediately called on Denious to say they thought these reprints were in poor taste, and he ceased his efforts to remind local citizens of their roots.

One man, a participant in some of those events, did make an effort to remind the people of Dodge of their heritage—not the violence, but the town's debt to the cowboy and the longhorn. He was Dr. O. H. Simpson, a dentist who moved to Dodge in 1885 and became something of a town character because of his habit of wearing a plug hat. As a hobby Dr. Simpson sculptured. One of his works was a cement figure of a cowboy, modeled for Dr. Simpson by Joe Sughrue, a town policeman. For years it stood on

City Hall in Dodge. *Courtesy Kansas Historical Society.*

the lawn of the city hall bearing a bronze plaque that stated, "On the ashes of my campfire this city is built." Another sculpture by Dr. Simpson was two steer heads; these bore the inscription, "My trails have become your highways." In smaller print was the reminder, "Seven million head of Longhorns marketed from Dodge, 70's-80's." Both of these eventually were placed on Boot Hill.

Neither of these efforts glorified the sordid aspects of the town's history, however, and they were acceptable. But they came at a time when there was a national trend to whitewash the gambler-lawmen and saloonkeeper-lawmen of the West. Earle Forrest in 1927 published an article in *Fur-Game-Fish* entiled "Wicked Dodge, Capital of the Old West." This was followed by other articles, such as Stuart Lake's "A Call to Dodge City" and "Straight-Shooting Dodge," William M. Raines's and Will C. Barnes's "Hell Roaring Dodge," and Owen P. White's "Man of War" (an article about Luke Short).[1] Books appeared with the same theme: Fred E. Sutton's *Hands Up*, Billy Breckinridge's *Helldorado*, Walter Noble Burns's *Tombstone: An Iliad of the Southwest*, and Stuart Lake's *Wyatt Earp: Frontier Marshal*.[2] This was the age of Zane Gray novels, pulp magazines containing stories about the real West, and the two- and three-reel Western movie.

Because of this climate, the city fathers planned a "Last Roundup" celebration to honor the founders of their town at the dedication of the new city hall in November 1929. One of the by-products of this event was a plan for a revival service—and even a tabernacle—at Boot Hill in an effort to efface the town's reputation as a haven for evil men and women in its early days.[3]

Then came the 1930s, bringing with them the Depression and a love affair with the movies. When Jack L. Warner late in 1938 announced that his studio was going to make a picture entitled "Dodge City," starring Errol Flynn and Ann Sheridan (the "Oomph girl"), the residents of Dodge were so enthusiastic that the Chamber of Commerce sent a delegation to Hollywood, consisting of early-day pioneers Ham Bell and Dr. Claude McCarty, along with the lieutenant governor of Kansas and lesser dignitaries, to invite the studio to premiere the film in Dodge City, which by then was calling itself the "Cowboy Capital of the World." Jack Warner agreed with their request, and arranged numerous publicity stories and photographs of the visit. On April 1, 1939, 50,000 fans waited three hours at the Santa Fe depot for the train bringing the stars of the picture, Errol Flynn, Ann Sheridan, Humphrey Bogart, Hoot Gibson, Buck Jones, John Garfield, John Payne, and Alan Hale. That evening a mob gathered in front of the Dodge Theater to catch another glimpse of these glamorous beings from California. During the ceremonies Flynn accepted the key to the city and made brief remarks. This staged event was considered one of the most exciting moments in Dodge's history.

Other movies followed in short order, pictures such as "Gunfighter in Dodge City," starring Joel McCrea. Low-budget films, called "B" pictures, used Dodge as the location for the action, as did radio shows involving the West. Many of these pictures played in foreign countries, making the fame of Dodge City international. Because Dodge was accessible by train (it was on the San Fe line) and by highway (US 54 parallels the old Santa F il, while US 70 follows the Arkansas to Bent's Fort and Puebl lorado), tourists came to Dodge to see the site of so many "f s" events—most of which were invented by movie writers in Hollywood. This caused some businessmen in the city, as well as the staff of the Chamber of Commerce, to think of opening tourist "attractions." First to come to mind as such an attraction was Boot Hill, for as early as 1932 its potential had been demonstrated. That year, when a convention of Rotarians was scheduled to meet in Dodge, Dr. Simpson had cast some skulls, boots, and death masks; as a joke, he placed the cement death masks at the original site of Boot Hill and buried the boots and skulls, thereby creating mock graves. These proved to be the hit of the convention.

By 1947 the cement death masks, along with the mock boots and skulls, had long-since disappeared when ground-breaking ceremonies were held to begin the rebuilding of the cemetery along with a museum. The tombstones had long since rotted and the bodies had been moved, but this did not stop businessmen from erecting a full slate of headboards complete with catchy epitaphs (the same epitaphs can be read at Boot Hill in Tombstone and elsewhere in tourist centers across the West). To this site they also moved a "hanging tree," supposedly used to hang a rustler at nearby Horse Thief Canyon. The museum was tastefully arranged, containing genuine pioneer artifacts, many of them belonging to the Beeson family, along with a skeleton uncovered in 1950. This was followed by an annual Boot Hill festival, complete with an official song, "The Ballad of Boot Hill."[4] In the souvenir shop at the museum could be purchased such items as a volume of poetry entitled *Boot Hill*,[5] capguns and holsters, and plastic Indian artifacts manufactured in Hong Kong. According to the Kansas Business Magazine of May 1951, the "Annual Boot Hill Fiesta Pulls out Large Crowds at Dodge City."

The crowds grew even larger with the start of "Gunsmoke," one of the most successful programs in television history. Adapted from a radio program that had been on the air for several years, "Gunsmoke" was widely hailed for its "authenticity." It featured the continuing adventures of a United States Marshal, Matt Dillon, who killed or captured almost all the evil characters in the central part of the United States, aided by his faithful friend and deputy, Chester, the town doctor, and "Miss Kitty," keeper of the Long Branch saloon. Anyone with any knowledge of Western history quickly realized that the claims to authenticity were nothing more than a press agent's lie. Because of its success, however, "Gunsmoke" was imitated by a host of other Western television series, including one about Wyatt Earp.

Overlooked in Dodge City was the admonition by local citizens to editor Jess C. Denious in 1910 that they wanted to forget the raw past. Tourism added dollars to the pockets of almost every resident of the town by the 1960s, and Dodge had become, according to one writer, "A Good Town Living up to a Bad Name."[6] To capitalize on its new-found fame, one group of businessmen purchased land on the west side of Dodge to build what supposedly was a replica of the town in the 1870s but which looked very similar to the set on which "Gunsmoke" was filmed. This featured a restaurant, shops, a theater, "souvenir" displays, stagecoach rides, and staged gunfights.

The visitor to Dodge City today will find a small town of approximately 18,000 people, most of them hard-working Americans. The fast-food chain stores dish up the same hamburgers, pizza, and fried chicken to be found anywhere else in America, just as chain motels provide plastic, airless, cheerless sleeping cubicles no different from rooms at other locations. Chain department and specialty stores sell the same lines of clothing, citizen's band radios, and washing machines, while gasoline stations dot the landscape. Even the junk yards are no different. And the center of town is dilapidated, with decaying buildings housing businesses struggling to compete with more modern shopping centers on the fringes of the city. Little about Dodge is extraordinary, just as the countryside surrounding it has farms growing wheat and ranches with pastures of grass no different from fields and pastures for hundreds of miles to the north or south. Dodge City is a Kansas—and Midwestern—small town, for unlike Tombstone and Deadwood it had a reason to continue when its boom period ended: to serve the farmers and ranchers in the area.

Yet Dodge City is extraordinary in that it is one of the few towns in America where a tourist can ask the average resident a question about local history and get an answer. The people of Dodge are knowledgeable, even proud, of their past—at least the violent aspect of it. Just as most of them can tell you about agricultural crops in the area and the kinds of cattle raised in the region, so they can recite facts about gunfights, gamblers, and cowboys. History is a local business, one good for the economy of the town. The gunfighters and peace officers may be fictional or, worse, bogus heroes, but school children can tell you how Wyatt Earp or Bat Masterson had a shootout at the corner of Front Street and Second Avenue in 1878.

History, one wit once declared, is a pack of lies previously agreed upon. Because of constant repetition in magazine, book, film, and teleplay, most Americans today believe in the myth of the Western "good guy" and Western outlaw. The West to them was a place where bad guys rode black horses and wore black hats: cattle rustlers, horse thieves, whiskey peddlers, gun runners, unscrupulous Indian agents, train robbers, Army deserters. The good guys rode white horses and wore white hats: sheriffs, deputies, town marshals, train detectives, cattle association agents, Wells Fargo men, Pinkerton operatives, U.S. Marshals. The two sides each had their following in the form of gang and posse, and they clashed in gunfights at high noon when men were ordered to leave town before sundown. This action transpired while the rest of the population sat in some nearby bar with nothing to do but drink, gamble, and act as witnesses to the violence. This was a lawless, restless, brawling, fighting, eye-gouging, ear-biting land, every man carrying a gun low on his hip, holster tied securely to thigh, ready to draw and fire with incredible speed and accuracy.

It never existed.

Yet modern Americans, beset by pressures and living in an insecure world, want—even need—to believe that such a place existed and that by visiting the site they can touch that less complicated era when a man met insult, real or fancied, with fist and gun. Old Town at the west side of Dodge City satisfies a need. Boot Hill cemetery with its fake gravestones satisfies a need. In a commercial society the tourist pays for his gratification. The result will not be as disastrous as the experience of the Dodge City Fire Department, which was called to a fire at a tavern in town. The firemen arrived to find the nearest fire hydrant across the street in front of an animal clinic, but when they attached a hose to it no water came out. A subsequent investigation disclosed that the hydrant was owned by the animal clinic, not the city, and that it was a fake placed there as a courtesy to visiting dogs.[7]

The traveler to Dodge City today quickly becomes aware that man has not yet conquered nature. He sees this in the vast distances, the big sky, and the great plains covered with wheat or grass. Nature still is capable of disrupting all local activity, just as it did 100 years ago. In 1911, for example, a storm dumped 14.5 inches of snow on the ground in thirty-six hours; a tornado struck the city in May 1949, while floods inundated the town in 1942 and again in 1965. Dodge still sits on a vast alluvial plain of rich soil that is subject to the seasonal rhythms of nature—soil still capable of producing grass, thereby linking the past and present and ensuring the future.

Notes

CHAPTER 1

1. Robert M. Wright, *Dodge City: The Cowboy Capital and the Great Southwest* (Wichita, Kansas: The Wichita Eagle, 1913), p. 70.
2. Herbert E. Bolton, *Coronado: Knight of Pueblos and Plains* (New York, 1949), p. 287.
3. Wright, *Dodge City*, pp. 71-72.
4. For details about these plains tribes, see Frank C. Lockwood, *The Apache Indians* (New York, 1938); Gordon Baldwin, *The Warrior Apaches* (Tucson: Dale S. King, 1966); Morris E. Opler, *An Apache Life-Way* (Chicago: University of Chicago Press, 1941); Ernest Wallace and E. Adamson Hoebel, *The Comanches: Lords of the South Plains* (Norman: University of Oklahoma Press, 1956).
5. For background details about the Santa Fe Trail, see Robert L. Duffus, *The Santa Fe Trail* (New York, 1930); Henry Inman, *The Old Santa Fe Trail* (New York, 1897); and Josiah Gregg, *Commerce of the Prairies*, ed. by Max L. Moorhead (Norman: University of Oklahoma Press, 1954).
6. See Buford Rowland (ed.), "Report of the Commissioners on the Road from Missouri to New Mexico, October, 1827," *New Mexico Historical Review*, XIV (July 1939), 213-29; Frederic A. Culmer, "Marking the Santa Fe Trail," *ibid.*, IX (January 1934), 78-93; and Kate L. Gregg (ed.), *The Road to Santa Fe* (Albuquerque: University of New Mexico Press, 1952).
7. Otis E. Young, Jr. (ed.), *The First Military Escort on the Santa Fe Trail, 1829; From the Journal and Reports of Major Bennet Riley and Lieuten-*

ant Philip St. George Cooke (Glendale, Cal.: Arthur H. Clarke Company, 1952).

8. George D. Brewerton, "In the Buffalo Country," *Harper's Magazine,* XXIV (June 1862), 457.

9. *Ibid.;* see also Robert W. Frazer, *Forts of the West* (Norman: University of Oklahoma Press, 1965), pp. 50-51.

10. Louise Barry, "Kansas before 1854," *Kansas Historical Collections,* L (1967), 26. See also Post Returns, Fort Atkinson, April 7, 1853, Records of the War Department; and Frazer, *Forts of the West,* pp. 50-51.

11. Wright, *Dodge City,* pp. 17-20.

CHAPTER 2

1. Grenville M. Dodge, *The Battle of Atlanta and Other Campaigns, Addresses, Etc.* (Council Bluffs, Iowa: Monarch Printing Company, 1911), pp. 63-64.

2. *Ibid.,* pp. 64-77; St. Louis *Western Journal of Commerce,* March 25, 1865.

3. *The War of the Rebellion: A Compilation of the Official Records of the Union and Confederate Armies,* 128 vols. (Washington, 1880-1901), Series I, XLVIII, 1204, 1224.

4. Grenville M. Dodge to Joseph B. Thoburn, October 24, 1910, in Archives, Kansas State Historical Society, Topeka.

5. Dodge, *Battle of Atlanta,* p. 102.

6. "Report on Barracks and Hospitals, with Descriptions of Military Posts," Surgeon General's Office, December 5, 1870, p. 301.

7. For additional details, see David K. Strate, *Sentinel to the Cimarron: The Frontier Experience of Fort Dodge, Kansas* (Dodge City, Kansas: Cultural Heritage and Arts Center, 1970).

8. Samuel J. Crawford, *Kansas in the Sixties* (Chicago: A. C. McClurg and Company, 1911), pp. 272-74.

9. Quoted in Wayne Gard, *The Great Buffalo Hunt* (New York, 1959), p. 87.

10. Wright, *Dodge City,* pp. 43-44.

11. Gard, *The Great Buffalo Hunt,* pp. 281-87, gives details of such episodes.

12. J. Wright Mooar, as told to James W. Hunt, "Buffalo Days," *Holland's,* LII (February 1933), 10, 44.

13. Wright, *Dodge City,* pp. 33-34.

14. For information about buffalo hunters and buffalo hunting, see Gard, *The Great Buffalo Hunt;* Marie Sandoz, *The Buffalo Hunters: The Hide Men*

(New York, 1954); Ralph K. Andrist, *The Long Death: The Last Days of the Plains Indians* (New York, 1964); and Wayne Gard, "How They Killed the Buffalo," *American Heritage*, VII (August 1955), 35-39. An especially interesting and helpful first-hand account of this hunting is Joseph W. Snell (ed.), "Diary of a Dodge City Buffalo Hunter, 1872-1873," *Kansas Historical Quarterly*, XXXI (Winter 1965), 345-95.

15. For the story of the building of this railroad, see James Marshall, *Santa Fe: The Railroad that Built an Empire* (New York, 1945).
16. Letters Sent, Fort Dodge, Kansas, 1866-1882 (August 29, 1872), Records of the War Department, RG 94, National Archives. See also Frederick R. Young, *Dodge City: Up through a Century in Story and Pictures* (Dodge City, Kansas: Boot Hill Museum, Inc., 1972), pp. 12-13.
17. George W. Brown, "Kansas Indian Wars," *Kansas Historical Collections*, XVII (1926-1928), 134-39.
18. U.S. Statutes, XIV, 541-42, XVI, 557; and *House Misc. Doc. 45*, 47 Cong., 2 Sess., pt. 4, p. 301.
19. County Records, Ford County Court House, Dodge City, Kansas. See also Helen G. Gill, "The Establishment of Counties in Kansas," *Kansas Historical Collections*, VIII (1903-1904).
20. Ida Ellen Rath, "Dodge City Town Company," *Kansas Genealogical Society The Treesearcher*, XII (Winter 1970), 5-6, and (Spring 1970), 81-84.

CHAPTER 3

1. For more details, see Odie B. Faulk, "Ranching in Spanish Texas," *Hispanic-American Historical Review*, XLV (May 1965), 257-66.
2. Miguel Ramos Arizpe, *Report to the August Congress on National, Political, and Civil Conditions of the Provinces of Coahuila, Nuevo León, Nuevo Santander, and Texas of the Four Eastern Provinces of the Kingdom of Mexico*, trans. and ed. by Nettie Lee Benson (Austin: The University of Texas Press, 1950), p. 21.
3. Census Office, Department of the Interior, *Report on the Production of Agriculture, June 1, 1880* (Washington, 1883), p. 965.
4. For a discussion of this animal and its characteristics, see J. Frank Dobie, *The Longhorns* (Boston, 1941).
5. For details about the mustang, see J. Frank Dobie, *The Mustangs* (Boston, 1952).
6. Garnet M. and Herbert O. Brayer, *American Cattle Trails* (Bayside, N.Y.: Western Range Cattle Industry Study, 1952), p. 26; Dobie, *The Longhorns*, p. 11.

7. Brayer and Brayer, *American Cattle Trails*, pp. 45-47; Wayne Gard, *The Chisholm Trail* (Norman: University of Oklahoma Press, 1954), p. 37.

8. L. P. Brackett, *Our Western Empire, or the New West beyond the Mississippi* (Philadelphia: Bradley, Garretson and Company, 1881), p. 176.

9. Joseph G. McCoy, *Historic Sketches of the Cattle Trade of the West and Southwest* (Kansas City, Mo.: J. T. Reton and Co., 1874), p. 23; Joseph Nimmo, *Report of the Chief of the Bureau of Statistics on Range Cattle Traffic* (Washington, 1885), p. 31; "Opening Session of the First National Cattle Growers' Convention," *Parson's Memorial and Historic Magazine*, I (1885), 298.

10. McCoy, *Historic Sketches of the Cattle Trade*, p. 116.

11. Dee Brown and Martin F. Schmitt, *Trail Driving Days* (New York, 1952), p. 7.

12. J. L. Hill, *The End of the Cattle Trail* (Long Beach, Cal.: Geo. W. Moyle, n.d.), p. 21; Walter Prescott Webb, *The Great Plains* (Boston, 1931), p. 222; McCoy, *Historic Sketches of the Cattle Trade*, pp. 111-25, 168-69.

13. McCoy, *Historic Sketches of the Cattle Trade*, pp. 135-37.

14. *Ibid.*, pp. 245-49.

15. Brown and Schmitt, *Trail Driving Days*, p. 66.

16. Edwin H. Van Patten, "A Brief History of David McCoy and Family," *Journal of the Illinois State Historical Society*, XIV (1921), 126.

17. Quoted in Robert R. Dykstra, *The Cattle Towns* (New York, 1968), p. 41.

18. McCoy, *Historic Sketches of the Cattle Trade*, pp. 229-31, 250; Census Office, *Report on the Production of Agriculture, June 1, 1880*, p. 975; Gard, *The Chisholm Trail*, p. 250.

19. For economic aspects of trail driving, see Jimmy M. Skaggs, *The Cattle-Trailing Industry: Between Supply and Demand, 1866-1890* (Lawrence: The University Press of Kansas, 1973). This is an excellent study worthy of close attention.

20. Ernest Wallace, "The Comanches on the White Man's Road," *West Texas Historical Association Year Book*, XXIX (1953), 6-7.

21. J. Evetts Haley, "Texas Fever and the Winchester Quarantine," *The Panhandle-Plains Historical Review*, VIII (1935), 38-41.

22. "Quarantine Law of the State of Colorado," "Quarantine Law of the Territory of Wyoming," and "Recent Acts of the Territory of New Mexico in Regard to the Quarantining of Texas Cattle," quoted in Nimmo, *Range Cattle Traffic*, pp. 136, 137, 141-42.

23. Dobie, *The Longhorns*, p. 39.

24. For more details about the adventures of this immigrant, see Godfrey

Sykes, *A Westerly Trend* (Tucson: Arizona Pioneers Historical Society, 1944).

25. Dobie, *The Longhorns*, p. 88.

CHAPTER 4

1. Richard Irving Dodge, *Our Wild Indians: Thirty-three Years' Personal Experience among the Red Men of the Great West* (Hartford, Conn.: A. D. Worthington and Company, 1883), pp. 608-11.
2. Wright, *Dodge City*, p. 138.
3. Dodge City *Times*, February 1, March 15, 1879, January 22, March 10, 1881; Dodge City *Globe*, February 11, 1879, March 8, 1881.
4. Some of the business records of Robert M. Wright's store survive in the Kansas State Historical Society, Topeka.
5. Quoted in Wright, *Dodge City*, pp. 155-56.
6. Sandoz, *The Buffalo Hunters*, pp. 165-66.
7. *Ibid.*, p. 166.
8. Dodge, *Our Wild Indians*, p. 611.
9. Myra E. Hull, "Cowboy Ballads," *Kansas Historical Collections*, XXV (1939).
10. The saloon account book kept by Hoover is in the Kansas State Historical Society, Topeka. See also Gerald Gribble, "George M. Hoover: Dodge City Pioneer" (M.A. thesis, University of Wichita, 1940).
11. Quoted in Samuel Carter III, *Cowboy Capital of the World: The Saga of Dodge City* (New York, 1973), p. 38.
12. Dodge City *Globe*, June 4, 1878; Dodge City *Times*, June 8, 22, October 19, 1878; and Dodge City *Cowboy*, August 9, 23, September 6, 1884.
13. Wright, *Dodge City*, p. 141; see also Dodge City *Times*, September 1, 1877.
14. Dodge City *Globe*, February 17, 1879.
15. Ford County *Globe*, February 17, 1879.
16. Ford County *Globe*, September 2, 1879.
17. Quoted in Carter, *Cowboy Capital*, p. 121.
18. Dodge City *Times*, June 8, 1878.
19. *Ibid.*, September 1, 1877.
20. Wright, *Dodge City*, pp. 140-41.
21. Carter, *Cowboy Capital*, pp. 153-54.
22. Wright, *Dodge City*, p. 152.
23. Robert R. Dykstra, in his excellent *The Cattle Towns* (New York, 1968), p. 108, summarizes this information in a table. I consulted, as he did, the Bureau of the Census, *Classified Index of Occupations and Industries*

206

Dodge City

(Washington, D.C., 1960), pp. xv-xx, and agree with his groupings of occupations for statistical purposes.

CHAPTER 5

1. Quoted in Wright, _Dodge City_, p. 144.
2. This information can be found in table form in Dykstra, _The Cattle Towns_, pp. 249, 251. The original information is in the Kansas Township Census, 1875, for Ford County, Dodge Township, pp. 1-21; the United States Manuscript Census for 1880, Kansas, Ford County, City of Dodge City; and the Kansas Manuscript Census, 1885, Ford County, City of Dodge City (all in the Kansas State Historical Society in the original or on microfilm).
3. Dodge City _Globe-Republican_, June 30, 1898.
4. Wright, _Dodge City_, p. 165.
5. Carter, _Cowboy Capital_, pp. 249-50.
6. Wright, _Dodge City_, p. 249.
7. _Ibid._, pp. 215-16.
8. _Ibid._, p. 243.
9. Dodge City _Times_, June 9, 1877.
10. For additional details, see _Diamond Jubilee, 1885-1960_ (Dodge City: Sacred Heart Cathedral Parish, November 13, 1960).
11. Dodge City _Times_, June 8, 1878; and Carter, _Cowboy Capital_, pp. 176-77. The medical history of early Dodge is scattered through the newspapers, and can be studied in the Physicians Registry, Ford County Courthouse, Dodge City.
12. Dodge City Commercial Club, _Dodge City and Ford County, Kansas_ (Larned, Kans.: Tucker-Vernon Printing Company, 1911), p. 22.
13. For Foy's comments about his career in Dodge City, see Eddie Foy and A. F. Harlow, _Clowning through Life_ (New York, 1928). See also Martin J. Maloney, "The Frontier Theater," _Players Magazine_, XVI (December 1939), 6, 20; and Carter, _Cowboy Capital_, pp. 160-61, 200.
14. See the _Times_ and _Globe_ for the month of October 1878.
15. Wright, _Dodge City_, pp. 82-85.
16. Carter, _Cowboy Capital_, p. 202.
17. _Ibid._, p. 201.
18. Dodge City _Times_, May 12, 1877.
19. Wright, _Dodge City_, pp. 240-42.
20. For details, see pertinent copies of the _Times_, _Globe_, and _Democrat_ for the week of July 4, 1884. See also Ruby Basye, "Early Day Dodge Bullfight Enraged Only the Spectators," _Hutchinson News_, May 11, 1958.

21. Wright, *Dodge City*, pp. 206-7.
22. *Ibid.*, pp. 207-8.
23. *Ibid.*, pp. 243-45.
24. *Ibid.*, pp. 252-55.
25. Dodge City *Globe-Republican*, September 13, 1906.
26. Dodge City *Times*, September 29, 1877.
27. This episode is related in Andy Adams's classic *Log of a Cowboy* (Boston, 1893).

CHAPTER 6

1. Wright, *Dodge City*, p. 148.
2. Dodge City *Times*, September 1, 1877.
3. Quoted in Young, *Dodge City*, pp. 39-40.
4. Dodge City *Times*, May 19, 1877.
5. Told in Wright, *Dodge City*, p. 150.
6. George M. Hoover's account of this incident is in the Dodge City *Democrat*, June 19, 1903. Bob Wright, in his *Dodge City*, p. 166, agrees in the main with Hoover's description, but states that the black man's name was Tex.
7. Dodge City *Democrat*, June 19, 1903.
8. See Dodge City *Times*, May 5, 1878, and Ford County *Globe*, January 28, 1879. See also Robert E. Eagen, "Boothill Victims and What Happened to Them," Denver Westerner's *Brand Book* (1963), pp. 404-10; and Robert E. Eagen, "Dodge City's Boot Hill," *True West*, XII (September-October 1964), 45, 51-52.
9. Dodge City *Times*, January 12, 19, 1878, and Nyle H. Miller and Joseph W. Snell, *Great Gunfighters of the Kansas Cowtowns, 1867-1889* (Lincoln: University of Nebraska Press, 1963), pp. 23-32.
10. Dodge City *Times*, June 9, 1877.
11. *Ibid.*, and July 7, 1877.
12. Miller and Snell, *Great Gunfighters*, p. 186.
13. Dodge City *Times*, July 21, 1877.
14. For details about Earp's life, see Ed E. Bartholomew, *Wyatt Earp, 1848 to 1880: The Untold Story* (Toyahvale, Texas: Frontier Book Company, 1964); Glenn G. Boyer, *The Suppressed Murder of Wyatt Earp* (San Antonio: The Naylor Company, 1967); Olga W. Hall-Quest, *Wyatt Earp: Marshal of the Old West* (New York, 1956); and Stuart N. Lake, *Wyatt Earp: Frontier Marshal* (Boston, 1931).
15. Dodge City *Times*, June 16, 1877, August 10, 1878.
16. *Ibid.*, November 10, 1877. Wyatt Earp later asserted, "Bat Masterson

was elected by a two-to-one majority"; see Lake, *Wyatt Earp*, p. 191. Earp's memory in this instance was as faulty as when he recalled other details of his life.

17. Dodge City *Times*, January 19, 1878.
18. *Ibid.*, April 13, 1878; Ford County *Globe*, April 16, 1878.
19. Dodge City *Times*, July 13, 1878.
20. *Ibid.*, July 27, 1878; Ford County *Globe*, August 27, 1878.
21. Foy and Harlow, *Clowning Through Life*, pp. 97-98.
22. Ford County *Globe*, April 8, 1879.
23. For a complimentary assessment of Bat Masterson's career in Dodge, see George C. Thompson, *Bat Masterson: The Dodge City Years* (Topeka, Kans.: State Printer, 1943; Fort Hays Kansas State College Studies, General Series, Number 6).
24. Dodge City *Times*, April 14, 1881.
25. Ford County *Globe*, April 19, 1881. This article was entitled, "The Festive Revolver: Again its Musical Voice is Heard in the Land."
26. A copy of these regulations was printed in the Dodge City *Times*, June 22, 1882.
27. The original copy of this information is in the Governors' Correspondence file, Archives Division, Kansas State Historical Society; a copy is in Miller and Snell, *Great Gunfighters*, pp. 378-80.
28. *Ibid.*, pp. 380-84.
29. *Ibid.*, pp. 384-413. See also Dodge City *Times*, November 20, 1883.
30. *Ibid.*, September 20, 1883.
31. *Globe Live Stock Journal*, July 22, August 5, 1884. Dave Mather reportedly was a descendant of Cotton Mather, the noted Puritan preacher of colonial New England.

CHAPTER 7

1. Quoted in Young, *Dodge City*, p. 124.
2. *House Executive Document* 78, 45 Cong., 2 Sess., 4-7.
3. For details see *House Report* 723, 46 Cong., 2 Sess., Bill 3191, 1-3; *House Executive Document* 195, 47 Cong., 1 Sess., 1-5; *Senate Executive Document* 73, 51 Cong., 1 Sess., 6; George L. Anderson, "The Administration of Federal Land Laws in Western Kansas, 1880-1890: A Factor in Adjustment to a New Environment," *Kansas Historical Quarterly*, XX (November 1952), 249.
4. *House Executive Document* 225, 47 Cong., 1 Sess., 7; Wright, *Dodge City*, p. 328; and *Senate Executive Document* 98, 49 Cong., 1 Sess., 1.
5. See David Strate, *Sentinel to the Cimarron: The Frontier Experience of*

Fort Dodge, Kansas (Dodge City: Cultural Heritage and Arts Center, 1970), pp. 114-17.
6. For details about this trade, see Gard, *The Great Buffalo Hunt*, pp. 295-99.
7. *Laws of Kansas* (1877), pp. 241-43.
8. *Ibid.*, January 20, February 3, 1880.
9. *Ibid.*, February 10, 17, 1880; Dodge City *Times*, February 14, 28, 1880.
10. Ford County *Globe*, April 23, 1878.
11. *Ibid.*, November 19, 1878, March 21, 28, August 8, 1882; Dodge City *Times*, August 31, December 21, 1878, March 23, 30, December 7, 1882.
12. Ford County *Globe*, April 8, 15, 1884; Dodge City *Times*, April 10, 1884.
13. *Laws of Kansas* (1885), 308-11; Dodge City *Times*, March 12, 1885.
14. Dodge City *Globe*, December 1, 1885.
15. *Ibid.*, August 18, 1885.
16. Dodge City *Democrat*, July 18, 1885.
17. Dodge City *Globe Live Stock Journal*, April 21, June 9, 1885.
18. J. C. Strang to J. A. Martin, July 5, 1885, Governors' Correspondence (General), Kansas State Historical Society, Topeka.
19. Martin to Wright, Governors' Letters, LXII, 127-37; Wright to Martin, Governors' Correspondence (General), Kansas State Historical Society, Topeka.
20. Dodge City *Times*, November 5, 12, December 3, 1885; Dodge City *Globe*, December 1, 8, 1885. This suit was not settled until 1887—at which time the court ruled in favor of the defendants, ruling the election legal.
21. These events are summarized in Young, *Dodge City*, pp. 139-45; see also newspapers for the first two weeks of December 1885 for details about the fires.
22. For details, see Young, *Dodge City*, pp. 154-56.

CHAPTER 8

1. Stuart N. Lake, "A Call to Dodge City," *Saturday Evening Post*, CCIII (November 15, 1930), 102; Stuart N. Lake, "Straight-Shooting Dodge," *ibid.*, CCII (March 8, 1930), 24; Earle R. Forrest, "Wicked Dodge, Capital of the Old Wild West," *Fur-Fish-Game*, XLVI-XLVII (October 1927, February 1928); and Owen P. White, "Man of War," *Colliers*, XCVII (March 14, 1936), 42, 77-78.
2. Fred E. Sutton, *Hands Up!* (New York, 1927); William M. Breckinridge, *Helldorado* (Boston, 1928); Walter N. Burns, *Tombstone: An Iliad*

of the Southwest (Garden City, N.Y., 1927); and Stuart N. Lake, *Wyatt Earp: Frontier Marshal* (Boston, 1931).

3. *New York Times*, August 18, 1929.
4. Bob Bain, "The Ballad of Boot Hill" (New York: Round Table Music, 1959).
5. Josephine McIntire, *Boot Hill* (Boston, 1945), contains forty-five pages of verse about the cowboy era.
6. Bob Pearmon, "Dodge City: A Good Town Living Up to a Bad Name," *Kiwanis Magazine*, XLV (July 1960), 34-36, 43-44.
7. This Associated Press story appeared in the Stillwater (Oklahoma) *News-Press*, March 28, 1976.

Bibliography

MANUSCRIPT SOURCES

Consolidated Quartermaster Records, 1865-1882, Fort Dodge, Kansas. Records of the War Department, RG 94, National Archives.

County Records, Ford County. Courthouse, Dodge City, Kansas.

Ford County Medical Society Records. Dodge City, Kansas.

George M. Hoover Account Books. Archives Division, Kansas State Historical Society, Topeka.

Governors' Correspondence. Archives Division, Kansas State Historical Society, Topeka.

Gribble, Gerald. "George M. Hoover: Dodge City Pioneer." M.A. thesis, University of Wichita, 1940.

Kansas Manuscript Census, 1885. Archives Division, Kansas State Historical Society, Topeka.

Kansas Township Census, 1875. Archives Division, Kansas State Historical Society, Topeka.

Post Returns, Fort Atkinson, Kansas. Records of the War Department, RG 94, National Archives.

Post Returns, Fort Dodge, 1866-1882. Records of the War Department, RG 94, National Archives.

Special Orders, Fort Dodge, Kansas, 1866-1882. Records of the War Department, RG 94, National Archives.

Robert M. Wright Store Records. Archives Division, Kansas State Historical Society, Topeka.

Sorenson, Conner. "A History of Irrigation in the Arkansas River Valley in Western Kansas, 1880-1910." M.A. thesis, University of Kansas, 1968.

Surgeon General's Office Records. Records of the War Department, RG 94, National Archives.

United States Manuscript Census, Kansas, 1880. Copy in Kansas State Historical Society, Topeka.

GOVERNMENT DOCUMENTS

Bureau of the Census. *Classified Index of Occupations and Industries.* Washington, D.C., 1960.

————. *Report on the Production of Agriculture, June 1, 1880.* Washington, D.C., 1883.

House Executive Document 78, 45 Cong., 2 Sess.

House Executive Document 195, 47 Cong., 1 Sess.

House Executive Document 225, 47 Cong., 1 Sess.

House Miscellaneous Document 45, 47 Cong., 2 Sess., Part 4.

House Report 723, 46 Cong., 2 Sess., Bill 3191.

Laws of Kansas, 1877, 1885.

Nimmo, Joseph. *Report of the Chief of the Bureau of Statistics on Range Cattle Traffic.* Washington, D.C., 1885.

Senate Executive Document 98, 49 Cong., 1 Sess.

Senate Executive Document 73, 51 Cong., 1 Sess.

The War of the Rebellion: A Compilation of the Official Records of the Union and Confederate Armies. 128 Vols. Washington, D.C., 1880-1901.

NEWSPAPERS

Dodge City *Democrat.*

Dodge City *Kansas Cowboy.*

Dodge City *Times.*

Ford County *Globe.*

Hutchinson (Kansas) *News.*

Junction City (Kansas) *Smoky Hill and Republican Union.*

Leavenworth (Kansas) *Daily Commercial.*

New York Times.
Stillwater (Oklahoma) *News-Press.*
St. Louis *Western Journal of Commerce.*
Washington, D.C.. *Evening Star.*

BOOKS

Adams, Andy. *Log of a Cowboy.* Boston, 1893.
Andrist, Ralph K. *The Long Death: The Last Days of the Plains Indians.* New York, 1964.
Arizpe, Miguel Ramos. *Report to the August Congress on National, Political, and Civil Conditions of the Provinces of Coahuila, Neuvo León, Nuevo Santander, and Texas of the Four Eastern Provinces of the Kingdom of Mexico,* trans. and ed. by Nettie Lee Benson. Austin: University of Texas Press, 1950.
Baldwin, Gordon. *The Warrior Apaches.* Tucson: Dale S. King, 1966.
Bartholomew, Ed E. *Wyatt Earp, 1848 to 1880: The Untold Story.* Toyahville, Texas: Frontier Book Company, 1964.
Bolton, Herbert E. *Coronado: Knight of Pueblos and Plains.* New York, 1949.
Boyer, Glenn G. *The Suppressed Murder of Wyatt Earp.* San Antonio: The Naylor Company, 1967.
Brackett, L. P. *Our Western Empire, or the New West beyond the Mississippi.* Philadelphia: Bradley, Garretson and Company, 1881.
Brayer, Garnet M. and Herbert O. *American Cattle Trails.* Bayside, N.Y.: Western Range Cattle Industry Studies, 1952.
Breckinridge, William M. *Helldorado.* Boston, 1928.
Brown, Dee, and Martin F. Schmitt. *Trail Driving Days.* New York, 1952.
Burns, Walter N. *Tombstone: An Iliad of the Southwest.* Garden City, N.Y., 1927.
Carey, Henry L. *The Thrilling Story of Famous Boot Hill and Modern Dodge City.* Dodge City: H. Etrick Printers, 1937.
Carter, Samuel, III. *Cowboy Capital of the World: The Saga of Dodge City.* New York, 1973.
Cox, William A. *Luke Short and His Era.* New York, 1961.
Crawford, Samuel J. *Kansas in the Sixties.* Chicago: A. C. McClurg and Company, 1911.

Diamond Jubilee, 1885-1960. Dodge City: Sacred Heart Cathedral Parish, 1960.

Dobie, J. Frank. *The Longhorns.* Boston, 1941.

———. *The Mustangs.* Boston, 1952.

Dodge, Richard I. *Our Wild Indians: Thirty-three Years' Personal Experience among the Red Men of the Great West.* Hartford, Conn.: A. D. Worthington and Company, 1883.

Dodge, Grenville M. *The Battle of Atlanta and Other Campaigns, Addresses, Etc.* Council Bluffs, Iowa: Monarch Printing Company, 1911.

Drago, Harry S. *Great American Cattle Trails: The Story of the Old Cow Paths of the East and the Longhorn Highways of the Plains.* New York, 1965.

Duffus, Robert L. *The Santa Fe Trail.* New York, 1930.

Dykstra, Robert L. *The Cattle Towns.* New York, 1968.

Foy, Eddie, and A. F. Harlow. *Clowning Through Life.* New York, 1928.

Frazer, Robert W. *Forts of the West.* Norman: University of Oklahoma Press, 1965.

Gard, Wayne. *The Chisholm Trail.* Norman: University of Oklahoma Press, 1954.

———. *The Great Buffalo Hunt.* New York, 1959.

Gregg, Josiah. *Commerce of the Prairies,* ed. by Max L. Moorhead. Norman: University of Oklahoma Press, 1954.

Gregg, Kate L. (ed.). *The Road to Santa Fe.* Albuquerque: University of New Mexico Press, 1952.

Haines, Francis. *The Buffalo.* New York, 1970.

Hall-Quest, Olga W. *Wyatt Earp: Marshal of the Old West.* New York, 1956.

Hammond, Dorothy M., and George Hendricks. *The Dodge City Story.* Indianapolis: Bobbs-Merrill, 1964.

Hill, J. L. *The End of the Cattle Trail.* Long Beach, Cal.: George W. Moyle, n.d.

Inman, Henry. *The Old Santa Fe Trail.* New York, 1897.

Jahns, Pat. *The Frontier World of Doc Holliday.* New York, 1957.

Lake, Stuart N. *Wyatt Earp: Frontier Marshal.* Boston, 1931.

Lockwood, Frank C. *The Apache Indians.* New York, 1938.

Lowther, Charles C. *Dodge City, Kansas.* Philadelphia: Dorance and Co., 1940.

Marshall, James. *Santa Fe: The Railroad That Built an Empire*. New York, 1945.

McCoy, Joseph G. *Historic Sketches of the Cattle Trade of the West and Southwest*. Kansas City, Mo.: J. T. Reton and Co., 1874.

McIntire, Josephine. *Boot Hill*. Boston, 1945.

Miller, B. S. *Ranch Life in Southern Kansas and the Indian Territory as Told by a Novice: How a Fortune Was Made in Cattle*. New York, 1896.

Miller, Nyle H., and Joseph W. Snell. *Great Gunfighters of the Kansas Cowtowns, 1867-1886*. Lincoln: University of Nebraska Press, 1963.

Opler, Morris E. *An Apache Life-Way*. Chicago: University of Chicago Press, 1941.

Rath, Ida Ellen. *Early Ford County*. Newton, Kans.: Mennonite Press, 1964.

————. *The Rath Trail*. Wichita: McCormick-Armstrong, 1961.

Sandoz, Mari. *The Buffalo Hunters: The Hide Men*. New York, 1954.

Schmidt, Heinie. *Ashes of My Campfire*. Dodge City: Journal Inc., 1952.

Skaggs, Jimmy M. *The Cattle-Trailing Industry: Between Supply and Demand, 1866-1890*. Lawrence: The University Press of Kansas, 1973.

Strate, David K. *Sentinel to the Cimarron: The Frontier Experience of Fort Dodge, Kansas*. Dodge City: Cultural Heritage and Arts Center, 1970.

Streeter, Floyd B. *Prairie Trails and Cow Towns*. Boston, 1936.

Sutton, Fred E. *Hands Up!* New York, 1927.

Swessinger, Earl A. *Texas Trail to Dodge City*. San Antonio: The Naylor Company, 1950.

Sykes, Godfrey. *A Westerly Trend*. Tucson: Arizona Pioneers' Historical Society, 1944.

Thompson, George G. *Bat Masterson: The Dodge City Years*. Topeka, Kans.: State Printer, 1943; Fort Hays Kansas State College Studies, General Series Number 6.

Tilghman, Zoe A. *Marshal of the Last Frontier*. Glendale, Cal.: Arthur H. Clarke, 1949.

Vernon, Joseph S. *Dodge City and Ford County, Kansas: A History of the Old and a Story of the New*. Larned, Kans.: Tucker-Vernon Publishing Company, 1911.

Vestal, Stanley. *Queen of Cowtowns: Dodge City.* New York, 1952.
Wallace, Ernest, and E. Adamson Hoebel. *The Comanches: Lords of the South Plains.* Norman: University of Oklahoma Press, 1956.
Webb, Walter P. *The Great Plains.* Boston, 1931.
Wright, Robert M. *Dodge City: The Cowboy Capital and the Great Southwest.* Wichita: The Wichita Eagle, 1913.
Young, Frederick R. *Dodge City: Up Through a Century in Story and Pictures.* Dodge City: Boot Hill Museum, Inc., 1972.
Young, Otis E., Jr. (ed.). *The First Military Escort on the Santa Fe Trail: From the Journal and Reports of Major Bennet Riley and Lieutenant Philip St. George Cooke.* Glendale, Cal.: Arthur H. Clarke, 1952.

ARTICLES

Anderson, George L. "The Administration of Federal Land Laws in Western Kansas, 1880-1890: A Factor in Adjustment to a New Environment," *Kansas Historical Quarterly,* XX (November 1952), 233-51.
"Annual Boot Hill Fiesta Pulls Out Large Crowd at Dodge City," *Kansas Business Magazine,* XIX (May 1951), 18.
Bain, Bob. "The Ballad of Boot Hill," New York: Round Table Music, 1959.
Barry, Louise. "Kansas Before 1854," *Kansas Historical Collections,* L (1967), 13-64.
Brewerton, George D. "In the Buffalo Country," *Harper's Magazine,* XXIV (June 1862), 457.
Brown, George W. "Kansas Indian Wars," *Kansas Historical Collections,* XVII (1926-1928), 134-39.
Culmer, Frederic A. "Marking the Santa Fe Trail," *New Mexico Historical Review,* IX (January 1934), 78-93.
"Dodge City: The Buckle on the Kansas Wheat Belt," Atchison, Topeka and Santa Fe *Earth,* XXVI (May 1929), 1-2.
Eagen, Robert E. "Boothill Victims and What Happened to Them," Denver Westerners *Brand Book* (1963), 404-10.
———. "Dodge City's Boot Hill," *True West,* XII (September-October 1964), 45, 51-52.
Faulk, Odie B. "Ranching in Spanish Texas," *Hispanic-American Historical Review,* XLV (May 1965), 257-66.

Bibliography 217

Forrest, Earle R. "Wicked Dodge: Capital of the Old West," *Fur-Fish-Game*, XLVI-XLVII (October 1927, February 1928).

Gard, Wayne. "How They Killed the Buffalo," *American Heritage*, VII (August 1955), 35-39.

Gill, Helen G. "The Establishment of Counties in Kansas," *Kansas Historical Collections*, VIII (1903-1904), 449-72.

"Gunsmoke T.V. Stars Matt Dillon, Kitty and Doc, in Dodge City for Two Day Celebration," *Kansas!*, XIII (November-December 1958), 11-13.

Haley, J. Evetts. "Texas Fever and the Winchester Quarantine," *Panhandle-Plains Historical Review*, VIII (1935), 37-53.

Hull, Myra E. "Cowboy Ballads," *Kansas Historical Collections*, XXV (1939), 35-60.

King, Henry. "Over Sunday in New Sharon," *Scribner's Magazine*, XIX (March 1880), 768.

Lake, Stuart N. "Straight-Shooting Dodge," *Saturday Evening Post*, CCII (March 8, 1930), 24-25, 145-48.

———. "A Call to Dodge City," *Saturday Evening Post*, CCIII (November 15, 1930), 16-17, 98-104.

Little, E. C. "Round Table of Dodge City: Border Men, Knights-Errant Who Surpassed the Achievements of Heroes of Romance," *Everybody's Magazine*, VII (November 1902), 432.

Maloney, Martin J. "The Frontier Theater," *Players Magazine*, XVI (December 1939), 6, 20.

Mooar, J. Wright. "Buffalo Days" (as told to James W. Hunt), *Holland's*, LII (February 1933), 10.

Morris, D. M. "Dodge City, Kansas," *Kansas Magazine*, IV (September 1910), 89.

"Opening Session of the First National Cattle Growers' Convention," *Parsons' Memorial and Historic Magazine*, I (1885), 298.

Paxson, F. L. "The Cow Country," *American Historical Review*, XXII (1916), 65-82.

Pearmon, Bob. "Dodge City: A Good Town Living Up to a Bad Name," *Kiwainis Magazine*, XLV (July 1960), 34-36, 43-44.

Rath, Ida E. "Dodge City Town Company," Kansas Genealogical Society *The Treesearcher*, XII (Winter 1970, Spring 1970), 4-6, 81-84.

Rowland, Buford. "Report of the Commissioners on the Road from

Missouri to New Mexico, 1827," *New Mexico Historical Review*, XIV (July 1939), 213-29.

Schaefer, Jack. "The Legend of Dodge City," *Holiday*, XXIII (May 1958), 88-89, 102-6.

Snell, Joseph W. (ed.). "Diary of a Dodge City Buffalo Hunter, 1872-1873," *Kansas Historical Quarterly*, XXXI (Winter 1965), 349-95.

Van Patten, Edwin H. "A Brief History of David McCoy and Family," *Journal* of the Illinois State Historical Society, XIV (1921), 121-35.

Wallace, Ernest. "The Comanches on the White Man's Road," West Texas Historical Association *Year Book*, XXIX (1953), 3-32.

Index